MOLTO GUSTO

MOLTO GUSTO

Easy Italian Cooking at Home

MARIO BATALI

and MARK LADNER

PHOTOGRAPHY BY
Quentin Bacon

ART DIRECTION BY
Douglas Riccardi and Lisa Eaton

An Imprint of HarperCollins Publishers

HarperCollins books may be purchased for educational, business, or sales promotional use. For information, please write: Special Markets Department, HarperCollins Publishers, 10 East 53rd Street, New York, NY 10022.

FIRST EDITION

Design by Memo Productions, NY

Library of Congress Cataloging-in-Publication Data has been applied for.

ISBN: 978-0-06-192432-3

10 11 12 13 14   ID/WCT   10 9 8 7 6 5 4 3 2 1

THIS BOOK IS DEDICATED TO

SUSI, BENNO & LEO

for whom *gusto* is a way of life — MARIO

I WOULD LIKE TO THANK MY FAMILY,

CHRISTINE, RILEY & JASPER,

for their support and patience — MARK

Contents

Acknowledgments

I would like to give special thanks to the following heroes in my funny world:

To **SUSI, BENNO,** and **LEO,** who keep me happy with smiles and wit throughout every single day of our lives

To **JOE BASTIANICH,** my business partner, and the playahz on our teams at all of B&B Hospitality Group, whose work gives us inspiration and keeps the humor flowing

To **PAMELA LEWY,** my communications director, whose diligence and intelligence keep the wheels on the whole bus, and other buses too

To **JUDITH SUTTON,** for making a book out of our chicken scratches and for testing the recipes for the real world

To **LISA EATON** and **DOUGLAS RICCARDI,** for all of the damn beauty and thought

To chef **DAN DROHAN,** for running Otto smoothly and at full tilt all of the time

To chef **MEREDITH KURTZMAN,** for the sweet stuff and constant thought in the cool world of desserts

To **DENNIS MULALLY** and the core of the Otto staff, for making Otto Pizzeria every day

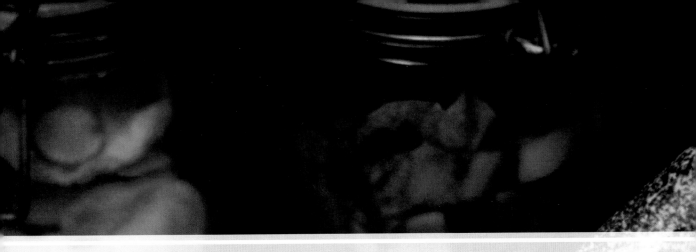

To **QUENTIN BACON** and **LAUREN VOLO**, for wisdom, velocity, and beauty of image

To **PAMELA DUNCAN SILVER**, **PAOLA RAMIREZ**, and **KARIN OLSEN**, for plates, settings, and thoughts

To **DANIEL HALPERN**, **GINNY SMITH**, **RACHEL BRESSLER**, **JOHN JUSINO**, and **LUCY ALBANESE** at Ecco, for being the successful ones in their strange business

To **JOHN FARBER**, for thoughtful and sage advice and follow-through

To **DARCIE PURCELL**, for helping build the mountain and the Mario Batali Foundation

To **TONY GARDNER**, my agent, for watching the deal, and to **CATHY FRANKEL**, my lawyer, for watching everyone else

To **JUAN MIGUEL** and **JULIE PANEBIANCO**, for unswerving support and humor

To my partners at **COPCO**, **CROCS**, **VIC FIRTH**, **GIA RUSSA**, **DCI CHEESE**, **ERNST BENZ**, and **FRAPPÉ PRODUCTIONS**, for vision and perseverance

To **JIM HARRISON**, for the voice in my head asking me about naps and lunchtime

From Mark

I would like to thank my partners, Mario, Joe, and Jason, for their inspiration and vision

And I would like to thank everyone at Lupa, Otto, and Del Posto for their dedication and hard work!

Introduction

I have written and spoken perhaps too many words about Italian food and how and why I translate its inherent excellence and deliciousness to the American table. I have been on and in several thousand television shows and explained to a very large audience the philosophy of the Italian family, the importance of the table in daily life, and the significance of regional variations and the fierce respect and love for these regional differences from town to town—and even from home to home on the same street. I have and will continue to espouse this Italian strategy, and I love to interpret it and illuminate it for the many of us who are Italians, whether or not we were born there—that is, we have ancestral roots there—and for the many of us who merely want to be Italians, at least at the dinner table.

Us is a big word these days, and I do not use it lightly. Who are we? By *we,* I mean those like-minded individuals who seek out the delicious, the traditional, the innovative, the unique, and the geo-specific in the world of nutrition and pleasure at the table, almost always in the company of others like us or of the same mind. We like to shop for food and prepare it, we like to braise, roast, poach, and steam. We have some but not all of the equipment we have seen on the cooking shows, and we have access to many great regional ingredients in our own towns. We lust after the first asparagus of the season, we anxiously await the first local strawberries or cherries, and we are not afraid of either simple or many-step recipes. We love the change from merely slicing tomatoes and adding salt to complex braising as summer fades and autumn slides in. We sometimes plan menus for get-togethers weeks, or even a month or two, in advance. We are the cooks the houseware companies want to sell to. We are the readers of *Food & Wine* and *Bon Appétit* and of the local newspaper food pages, and we are the core audience of anything written by Michael Pollan, Mark Bittman, and Alice Waters. But we are not snobs or elitists, and we love it when other people cook for us. We like simple food.

In the last few years, the idea that there are social costs associated with the decisions we make at the grocery store and at the table has become quite compelling. At all of the restaurants I own, we

What seems to be all the rage in the smart world of foodies is simply an extension of the traditional Italian table . . .

have spent significant time thinking these decision-based costs through, and we have taken many steps to prove our pro-planet resolve, never at the loss of flavor and pleasure, but often in the face of seemingly significant profit motives. Among other things, we no longer sell imported bottled water, a reflection of our thoughts on the use of limited resources in energy and other raw materials we consider important. We have become "green-certified" at nearly every location, installing efficient lighting, composting our carbon-based waste, and recycling all plastic and glass. We are buying hormone-free meat and poultry products, and in many cases we have driven our menus to a place with less and less protein as the main event. At no place is this drive toward less protein more evident than at Otto Pizzeria Enoteca. The idea that our protein-heavy diet has far-reaching

implications, including energy and resource management as well as global warming, may seem new, but the traditional agrarian European diet is actually anything but "hot off the press."

We created Otto Pizzeria for one basic reason, to give us a place to go with our kids that made sense in the "big three" for families: (1) to have fun; (2) to be able to find something the kids want to eat at the same place where the adults want to eat; and (3) to serve both adults and kids something that is good for them but, at the same time, delicious—without having to resort to the didacticism and sloganeering language that "health food" restaurants are trapped by. In the true world of Italian meal ideology, this is not as hard as it might seem when you look at that list: we simply created a menu that doesn't require a huge commitment to any particular or specific course. The typical meals may change from day to day, but most people have some vegetable antipasti and a leafy salad or two, maybe some cheeses or salumi, and then split a few pastas and a few pizzas and share a couple of gelati and coppette. I do not think that after our first year anyone even noticed that there are no standard meat- or fish-based main courses served in the restaurant. And if you have been paying attention to the current food brain-trust literati, it seems that our customers were ahead of the curve. Not really vegetarian, they've nonetheless been eating a diet heavy on vegetables, mostly leafy, with some grains thrown in, in the form of pasta and pizza, plus farro and legumes in salads, and very little protein from animals.

What you will certainly notice quite quickly is that this cookbook is radically different from all of the others I have written in its complete lack of traditional main courses. We do not serve any "meat and potatoes" plates at Otto, and we never have. What seems to be all the rage in the smart world of foodies is simply an extension of the traditional Italian table, where farming, foraging, and gardening have always yielded the bulk of the food in the daily diet, and where the occasional pig, chicken, or cow has been the exception to the rule. The health implications of this style of diet are no new shakes either, but I think that what you will note when dining on the following group of recipes is a kind of happy passing sense of content and fullness not associated with the consumption of a huge steak or chop. Most of the protein comes from small portions of cured meats, cheeses, and grains, with any animal protein as the flavoring and the bulk of the actual comestibles plant-based, whether leaf, stalk, flower, seed, or drupe. An ideal meal for several people from this book might consist of two or three vegetable antipasti, and a salad, followed by a pasta or two and a cheese course. Or maybe a plate of salumi and then some pizzas, with a couple of gelati and a coppetta or two.

The real trick is to let the market inspire you to buy and forage for the right things, then take them home and prepare them—and spend at least that amount of time enjoying them. You will notice that many of the recipes in this book are less than half a page long. This reflects the fact that they are indeed simple and a real part of the daily lives of many Italian people, who base a lot of their cooking and eating more on great products that they merely adorn.

But I do not want to weigh you down with a lot of political rigamarole. What is most important about food is the pleasure and nourishment it gives us. The sourcing is as significant a component of the process as the cooking, but let's not forget that the main event is not just to care for ourselves, but also to create energy for our constantly moving lives and our brains, and our laughing and singing and dancing and playing. So look at these recipes and ideas and think about smaller plates of food in a meal much less reliant on a big main course, yet still involving big beautiful flavors, and, most important, variation with the seasons. Many of the recipes are, in fact, organized by seasonal availability.

VEGETABLE ANTIPASTI

There is nothing that

inspires me more, no matter where I am in the world, than a visit to a local farmers' market. To see what the sweet earth is giving up to those who care enough to coax it into fruition is my main gauge of the greatness of a town or city in any society.

From London's Borough Market to the Boqueria in Barcelona and Rome's Campo dei Fiori to Pike Place Market in Seattle and the Union Square Greenmarket near my home in NYC, there is the constant source of inspiration driven by the fact that the general constituency of both purveyor and customer represents everything I love about great food and its potential. The single most exciting word in food for me is *geo-specificity.* If I can find something that is grown close to where I buy it (and plan on eating it), and it tastes like the smell of the wind on a rainy day in May or July or September, I have found something unique.

The recipes in this chapter are based on things we can find at our green-market in New York City, and they are generally so simple that I can for the first time put several recipes on a single page. (This is a new format for me and maybe for you too.) As usual, the best thing to do is go to the market and find the finest stuff, buy it, and bring it home. Then peruse the books you have—including this one—and find the simplest recipe you can for those ingredients. And then? Cook them and eat them with your friends and family!! It is the Italian way and the French way and the Spanish way and the Chinese way—I could go on and on describing the best food cultures from antiquity to the present. A series of four or five of these dishes might be a light snack or a brunch. Add a plate or two of salumi and cheeses, and you have a party. Add some of our fabulous homemade pizzas and a couple of pastas, followed by some gelati, and you have a bona-fide feast!

We have organized the recipes by season for the simple reason that that is how we think about all food, when it is at its most delicious, and most abundant, and least expensive. One of the great things about these vegetable dishes is that you can make just about all of them in advance and let them sit in the fridge overnight, or even for two or three nights (though if you are planning to make them ahead of time, it's really best if you do not add the acidic component of the dressing—e.g., vinegar, citrus juice, etc.— until shortly before serving them). In fact, most of them will get even better as the flavors marry whilst mingling in the darkness.

17

~ Radishes ~

WITH BUTTER DRESSING

RECIPE PAGE 27

18

Fresh Fava Beans

WITH RICOTTA SALATA

RECIPE PAGE 24

19

Shaved Asparagus

WITH
PARMIGIANO-REGGIANO

RECIPE PAGE 25

20

Artichokes with Grana Padano

RECIPE PAGE 26

21

**Chickpeas
with Leeks**

RECIPE PAGE 27

22

**Spring Peas
with Mint**

RECIPE OPPOSITE

Spring Peas
with Mint

SERVES 6 · PHOTO OPPOSITE

2 pounds peas in the pod, shelled,
   or 2 cups fresh peas

1 medium red onion, cut into dice about
   the same size as the peas

½ bunch fresh mint, leaves removed
   and torn into 2 or 3 pieces each

¼ cup Red Wine Vinaigrette
   (recipe follows)

Maldon or other flaky sea salt and
   coarsely ground black pepper

Combine the peas, onion, and mint in a
medium bowl and toss with the vinaigrette.
Season with salt and pepper and serve, or
let stand at room temperature for 1 hour to
bring out the flavors. *(The peas can be refrigerated for up to 1 day; bring to room temperature before serving.)*

RED WINE VINAIGRETTE
MAKES 1 CUP

¼ cup red wine vinegar, preferably Chianti

¼ cup sparkling water

½ cup extra virgin olive oil, preferably
   Ligurian

Whisk the vinegar, water, and olive oil
together in a small bowl. *(The vinaigrette can
be refrigerated for up to 5 days.)*

Fresh Fava Beans with Ricotta Salata

SERVES 6 · PHOTO PAGE 18

2 pounds young fava beans in the pod, shelled

Scant ¼ cup Lemon Vinaigrette (recipe follows)

Maldon or other flaky sea salt

A 3-ounce chunk of ricotta salata for grating

Coarsely ground black pepper

If the fava beans are young and tender, there is no need to peel them. It not, blanch the beans in a medium pot of boiling salted water for 30 seconds, just to loosen the skins. Drain, transfer to an ice bath to cool, and drain again. To peel the favas, pinch open the skin at one end of each bean and squeeze out the bean.

Toss the fava beans with the vinaigrette in a medium bowl and season with salt. Grate the ricotta over the favas, sprinkle pepper over the top, and serve immediately.

LEMON VINAIGRETTE

MAKES ¾ CUP

¼ cup fresh lemon juice

1 teaspoon lemon marmellata (marmalade) or a generous pinch of grated lemon zest

½ cup extra virgin olive oil, preferably Tuscan

Whisk the lemon juice, marmellata, and olive oil together in a small bowl. *(The vinaigrette can be refrigerated for up to 3 days.)*

Shaved Asparagus with Parmigiano-Reggiano

SERVES 6 · PHOTO PAGE 19

2 pounds medium asparagus, tough bottom ends snapped off

3 ounces Parmigiano-Reggiano, coarsely grated

Juice of 1 lemon

2 tablespoons warm water

¼ cup extra virgin olive oil

Maldon or other flaky sea salt and coarsely ground black pepper

Using a Benriner (Japanese mandoline) or other vegetable slicer, or a vegetable peeler, thinly shave the asparagus, making long diagonal shavings.

Put the Parmigiano in a large bowl and whisk in the lemon juice and warm water. Whisking constantly, slowly drizzle in the oil to make a loose emulsion. Add the asparagus and toss gently to coat. Season with salt if necessary and with pepper and serve.

Artichokes with Grana Padano

SERVES 6 · PHOTO PAGE 20

3 cups water

1 cup dry white wine

Juice of 2 lemons

2 pounds baby artichokes (about 16)

¼ cup coarsely chopped fresh basil,
    stems reserved

1 medium white onion, cut into ¼-inch dice

5 garlic cloves, smashed and peeled

1 bay leaf, preferably fresh

¼ cup extra virgin olive oil

Maldon or other flaky sea salt

Hot red pepper flakes

Tiny fresh mint leaves for garnish (optional)

Thinly sliced red onion for garnish (optional)

A 3-ounce chunk of grana padano cheese for
    shaving

Combine the water, wine, and lemon juice in a medium bowl. Pull off the tough outer leaves from each artichoke, then cut off the top ½ inch of the remaining leaves. Trim the bottom of the artichoke stem, then cut off the top outer layer of the stem with a paring knife. Transfer the artichokes to the lemon juice mixture as you work, to prevent oxidation.

Transfer the artichokes and their liquid to a medium pot; if necessary, add more water to cover the artichokes. Add the basil stems, onion, garlic, and bay leaf, put a pan lid on top of the artichokes to keep them submerged, and bring to a boil. Reduce the heat to a simmer and cook until the artichokes are tender (test the centers with the tip of a sharp knife), 10 to 15 minutes. Drain the artichokes, reserving the garlic, and let cool slightly; discard the basil stems and bay leaf.

Halve the artichokes lengthwise with a sharp knife. Chop or mash the garlic. Transfer the artichokes and garlic to a sauté pan, add the oil, and cook over medium heat, stirring occasionally, until the artichokes are very tender, 12 to 15 minutes. Season with salt and red pepper flakes and serve, or let stand at room temperature for up to 1 hour to bring out the flavors. *(The artichokes can be refrigerated for up to 3 days; bring to room temperature before serving.)*

To serve, transfer the artichokes to a bowl, scatter the mint leaves and red onion, if using, over them, and, using a vegetable peeler, shave the cheese over the top.

Chickpeas with Leeks

SERVES 6 · PHOTO PAGE 21

Two 15-ounce cans chickpeas, rinsed and drained

1 cup Leek Ragu (page 93)

½ cup extra virgin olive oil

Maldon or other flaky sea salt

1 to 2 teaspoons hot red pepper flakes

Combine the chickpeas and leeks in a large bowl. Add the oil, salt to taste, and red pepper flakes, tossing vigorously to combine. Serve, or let stand at room temperature for 1 hour to bring out the flavors. *(The chickpeas can be refrigerated for up to 3 days; bring to room temperature before serving.)*

Radishes with Butter Dressing

SERVES 6 · PHOTO PAGE 17

6 tablespoons unsalted butter, melted

2 tablespoons very warm water

¼ cup extra virgin olive oil

1 pound radishes, preferably French Breakfast radishes, trimmed and halved lengthwise

Maldon or other flaky sea salt

Whisk the butter, water, and oil together in a small bowl until emulsified. Put the radishes on a serving plate, drizzle with the dressing, season with salt, and serve. Or serve the dressing alongside for dipping.

28

Green Beans

WITH CHARRED ONIONS

RECIPE PAGE 34

29

Farro
with Cucumbers

RECIPE PAGE 35

30

Cherry Tomatoes
WITH CRÈME FRAÎCHE
& CHIVES

RECIPE PAGE 35

31

Roasted Peppers with Capers

RECIPE PAGE 36

32

Hot & Cold Summer Squash

RECIPE PAGE 37

33

Fregula with Corn

RECIPE PAGE 46

Green Beans with Charred Onions

SERVES 6 · PHOTO PAGE 28

Kosher salt

1 pound young green beans or
haricots verts

2 medium sweet onions, such as Vidalia or
Walla Walla

1½ tablespoons balsamic vinegar

1½ tablespoons orange juice

2 tablespoons extra virgin olive oil

Maldon or other flaky sea salt

Bring 4 quarts of water to a boil in a large
pot and add 2 tablespoons kosher salt. Add
the beans and blanch until crisp-tender, 3
to 5 minutes. Drain in a colander and cool
under cold running water; drain well.

Halve the onions lengthwise and trim off
the ends. Cut lengthwise into ½-inch-wide
slices.

Heat a dry 12-inch sauté pan over medium-
high heat until very hot. Add the onions
and sauté until charred in spots but still
crunchy, 4 to 6 minutes. During the last
minute or so, add the beans, stirring and
tossing to warm them through. Transfer the
beans and onions to a large bowl.

Whisk the balsamic vinegar, orange juice,
and oil together in a small bowl. Pour over
the beans and onions, tossing to coat. Let
stand for at least 10 minutes, or up to
1 hour, before serving.

Sprinkle the beans with Maldon salt and
serve.

Farro with Cucumbers

SERVES 6 · PHOTO PAGE 29

8 ounces (about 1½ cups) farro, preferably "perlato," or semipearled, or wheat berries, picked over and rinsed

1 pound cucumbers, cut into ¼-inch dice

1 medium red onion, cut into ¼-inch dice

1 red finger chile or serrano chile, cut into tiny dice

⅓ cup packed fresh basil leaves, thinly sliced (chiffonade)

½ cup Red Wine Vinaigrette (page 23)

Maldon or other flaky sea salt

Combine the farro and water to cover by 2 inches in a large saucepan and bring to a simmer, skimming off the foam. Reduce the heat to a bare simmer and cook until the farro is just tender, about 25 minutes if using pearled farro, about 1½ hours if using whole-grain farro (or wheat berries).

Drain the farro and transfer to a large bowl. Add the cucumbers, onion, chile, and basil, mixing well. Add the vinaigrette, tossing well. Season well with salt and serve, or let stand at room temperature for 1 hour to bring out the flavors. *(The farro can be refrigerated for up to 3 days; bring to room temperature before serving.)*

Cherry Tomatoes with Crème Fraîche & Chives

SERVES 6 · PHOTO PAGE 30

12 ounces ripe cherry, grape, or pear tomatoes, halved

2 tablespoons sherry vinegar

Maldon or other flaky sea salt

6 tablespoons crème fraîche

¼ cup extra virgin olive oil, plus extra for drizzling

Fresh chive sticks for garnish

Put the tomatoes in a serving bowl and add the vinegar, tossing to coat. Season with salt, and let marinate for 10 minutes, tossing occasionally.

Combine the crème fraîche and oil in a medium bowl and whisk until the cream just holds a soft shape.

Garnish the tomatoes with dollops of the crème fraîche, drizzle with olive oil, sprinkle with chives, and serve.

Roasted Peppers with Capers

SERVES 6 · PHOTO PAGE 31

2 pounds red bell peppers (4 large)

2 pounds green bell peppers (4 large)

6 tablespoons extra virgin olive oil

6 garlic cloves, cut into thick slivers

¼ cup salt-packed capers, rinsed and soaked overnight in cold water (change the water several times)

¼ cup balsamic vinegar

Maldon or other flaky sea salt

1 teaspoon hot red pepper flakes, or to taste

Preheat the broiler. Rub the peppers all over with 2 tablespoons of the olive oil, put them on a baking sheet, and broil, turning often, until blistered and charred all over, 15 to 20 minutes. Transfer the peppers to a paper bag and seal tightly, or put them in a large bowl and cover tightly with plastic wrap. Allow to steam and cool for 10 minutes.

Peel the peppers, remove the cores and seeds, and cut the peppers into 1-inch-wide strips. Put in a medium bowl.

Combine the garlic and the remaining ¼ cup olive oil in a 10-inch sauté pan and warm over medium heat, stirring, until the garlic just starts to turn golden, 2 to 3 minutes. Remove from the heat.

Combine the capers and balsamic vinegar in a small bowl. Whisk in the garlic oil, with the garlic. Season with salt and red pepper flakes and whisk again.

Pour the vinaigrette over the peppers, turning gently to coat. Serve, or let stand at room temperature for 1 hour to bring out the flavors. *(The peppers can be refrigerated for up to 3 days; bring to room temperature before serving.)*

Note: This vinaigrette is also a great way to punch up jarred roasted piquillo peppers (see Sources, page 266).

Hot & Cold Summer Squash

SERVES 6 · PHOTO PAGE 32

5 tablespoons extra virgin olive oil

3 garlic cloves, smashed and peeled

2 pounds small zucchini and/or striped zucchini or yellow summer squash, sliced into ⅓-inch-thick rounds

½ cup minced tender parsley stems

Maldon or other flaky sea salt

2 tablespoons grated orange zest (use a Microplane or other rasp grater)

2 to 3 teaspoons hot red pepper flakes

¾ cup Pomì strained tomatoes, simmered until reduced by half

Heat a 12-inch sauté pan over medium heat until hot. Add 2 tablespoons of the olive oil, then add the garlic and sauté for 1 minute, or until golden brown. Add half of the zucchini and half of the parsley, season well with salt, and sauté until the zucchini is softened but not browned, about 7 minutes. Stir in 1 tablespoon of the orange zest and half of the red pepper flakes and transfer to a large bowl. Add 2 tablespoons oil to the pan and heat until hot, then add the remaining zucchini and parsley, season with salt, and sauté until the zucchini is softened but not browned. Stir in the remaining 1 tablespoon orange zest and red pepper flakes and add to the first batch of zucchini, tossing gently.

Add the tomato sauce to the zucchini and mix gently. Add the remaining tablespoon of oil, mixing gently. Let stand for at least 10 minutes, or up to 1 hour, before serving. *(The zucchini can be refrigerated for up to 3 days; serve chilled or at room temperature.)*

Brussels Sprouts with Mustard

SERVES 6 · PHOTO PAGE 39

2 pounds Brussels sprouts

4 ounces pancetta, cut into ¼-inch dice (ask for pancetta sliced ¼ inch thick when you buy it)

Maldon or other flaky sea salt

¼ cup black mustard seeds (see Sources, page 266)

Grated zest and juice of 1 lemon

3 tablespoons mustard oil (see Sources, page 266)

Preheat the broiler. Trim the stems of the Brussels sprouts and remove any discolored leaves. Slice the sprouts lengthwise in half and transfer to a large bowl.

Set a 10-inch sauté pan over medium heat, add the pancetta, and cook, stirring occasionally, until it has rendered some of its fat and is beginning to brown and caramelize, about 5 minutes.

Pour the pancetta and fat over the Brussels sprouts, tossing to coat. Season well with salt. Transfer to a baking sheet (set the bowl aside), spreading the sprouts out in a single layer. Broil 4 inches from the heat source, stirring occasionally, for 15 to 18 minutes, until lightly browned and just tender.

Return the Brussels sprouts to the bowl, add the mustard seeds, lemon zest and juice, and oil, and stir to mix. Taste and season with more salt if necessary. Serve, or let stand at room temperature for 1 hour to bring out the flavors. *(The Brussels sprouts can be refrigerated for up to 3 days; bring to room temperature before serving.)*

39

Brussels Sprouts with Mustard

RECIPE OPPOSITE

40
Broccoli with Pecorino Romano

RECIPE PAGE 47

41

Cauliflower
with Olives

RECIPE PAGE 48

42

Broccoli Rabe

WITH MOZZARELLA CREMA

RECIPE PAGE 49

43

**Lentils
with Pancetta**

RECIPE PAGE 49

44

White Beans

RECIPE PAGE 50

45
Broiled Pumpkin with Apples
RECIPE PAGE 51

Fregula with Corn

SERVES 6 · PHOTO PAGE 33

Kosher salt

½ pound (about 1⅓ cups) fregula

1 tablespoon extra virgin olive oil

1 cup fresh corn kernels

Maldon or other flaky sea salt

¼ cup thinly sliced scallions

2 tablespoons Lemon Vinaigrette (page 24)

Coarsely ground black pepper

Bring 4 quarts of water to a boil in a large pot and add 2 tablespoons kosher salt. Add the fregula and cook until al dente, 10 to 12 minutes. Drain well.

Meanwhile, heat a large cast-iron or other heavy skillet over high heat until smoking hot. Add the olive oil and heat until very hot, then add the corn and cook, stirring once or twice, until the kernels are charred in spots, about 2 minutes (watch out for popping corn kernels). Season with Maldon salt and cook, stirring, until just tender, another minute or so. Transfer to a large bowl and allow to cool.

Add the fregula and scallions to the corn, then add the vinaigrette and toss well. Season generously with Maldon salt and with pepper. Serve, or let stand at room temperature for 1 hour to bring out the flavors. *(The fregula can be refrigerated overnight; let come to room temperature before serving.)*

Broccoli with Pecorino Romano

SERVES 6 · PHOTO PAGE 40

Kosher salt

1 large bunch broccoli (about 1½ pounds)

½ cup coarsely grated pecorino romano

2 tablespoons warm water

2 tablespoons extra virgin olive oil

Maldon or other flaky sea salt and coarsely
ground black pepper

Bring a large pot of water to a boil and add
2 tablespoons kosher salt.

Cut off the thick broccoli stalks, and cut
the broccoli into 1-inch florets with about
1 inch of the tender stalks. Reserve the
stalks for another use. Add the broccoli to
the boiling water and blanch until crisp-
tender, about 3 minutes; do not overcook.
Drain in a colander and rinse under cold
water to stop the cooking; drain well and
pat dry.

Put the pecorino in a large bowl and whisk
in the warm water. Whisking constantly,
slowly drizzle in the oil to make a loose
emulsion. Add the broccoli and toss to
coat. Season with Maldon salt if necessary
and with pepper. Let stand for 30 minutes
before serving.

Cauliflower with Olives

SERVES 6 · PHOTO PAGE 41

1 medium head cauliflower (about
  2 pounds), trimmed, halved lengthwise,
  cored, and cut into bite-sized or smaller
  florets

3 tablespoons extra virgin olive oil

Maldon or other flaky sea salt and coarsely
  ground black pepper

½ cup pitted Kalamata olives

3 tablespoons salt-packed capers, rinsed and
  soaked overnight in cold water (change
  the water several times)

1½ teaspoons hot red pepper flakes
  (optional)

3 tablespoons lemon agrumato oil (see
  Sources, page 266), or 3 tablespoons
  extra virgin olive oil plus ½ teaspoon
  grated lemon zest

Preheat the broiler. Toss the cauliflower with the olive oil in a large bowl and season with salt and pepper. Spread out in a single layer on a large baking sheet (set the bowl aside) and broil 4 inches from the heat source, stirring occasionally, for 15 to 17 minutes, or until lightly charred in spots and just tender.

Return the cauliflower to the bowl, add the olives, capers, red pepper flakes, if using, and lemon oil, and toss to mix well. Taste and season with more salt and/or pepper if necessary. Serve, or let stand at room temperature for up to 1 hour to bring out the flavors. *(The cauliflower can be refrigerated for up to 3 days; bring to room temperature before serving.)*

Broccoli Rabe with Mozzarella Crema

SERVES 6 · PHOTO PAGE 42

Kosher salt

2 pounds broccoli rabe, stems trimmed

3 ounces fresh mozzarella, preferably with some of its brine

¼ cup extra virgin olive oil

Bring a large pot of water to a boil and add 2 tablespoons kosher salt. Add the broccoli rabe and blanch until crisp-tender, about 5 minutes. Drain in a colander and rinse under cold water to stop the cooking; drain well.

Coarsely chop the broccoli rabe. Transfer to a serving bowl.

Using a whisk, coarsely mash the mozzarella in a small bowl. Whisk in 2 tablespoons of the reserved brine (or warm water). Slowly add the olive oil, whisking until emulsified.

Spoon the mozzarella crema over the broccoli rabe, and serve.

Lentils with Pancetta

SERVES 6 · PHOTO PAGE 43

½ pound small lentils, preferably Castellucio (see Sources, page 266)

1 carrot, halved

1 onion, halved

1 celery rib, halved

2 tablespoons Dijon mustard

2 ounces pancetta, in one piece

2 tablespoons extra virgin olive oil

Maldon or other flaky sea salt and coarsely ground black pepper

Put the lentils in a medium pot, add water to cover by 2 inches, and bring to a simmer. Add the vegetables, mustard, and pancetta, reduce the heat, and simmer gently until the lentils are just tender, about 20 minutes. Drain, reserving ¼ cup of the cooking liquid, and transfer to a large bowl.

Remove the vegetables and pancetta from the lentils; discard the vegetables. Coarsely chop the pancetta and add to the lentils. Add just enough of the reserved cooking liquid to moisten the lentils, then add the oil and season with salt and pepper. Serve, or let stand at room temperature for 1 hour to bring out the flavors. *(The lentils can be refrigerated for up to 3 days; bring to room temperature before serving.)*

White Beans

SERVES 6 · PHOTO PAGE 44

8 ounces (about 1¼ cups) dried cannellini or other white beans, picked over and rinsed

1 carrot, halved

1 red onion, halved

1 celery rib, tough strings removed with a vegetable peeler and halved

4 garlic cloves, smashed and peeled

1 bay leaf, preferably fresh

1 sprig each fresh Italian parsley, sage, rosemary, and thyme

Maldon or other flaky sea salt

¼ cup extra virgin olive oil, or more to taste

1 tablespoon finely chopped fresh thyme

Coarsely ground black pepper

Put the beans in a large bowl or pot, add cold water to cover by 2 inches, and let soak for 12 to 24 hours.

Transfer the beans and soaking liquid to a medium pot, add enough water to cover by 2 inches, and bring to a simmer over medium-high heat, skimming off the foam. Add the vegetables, garlic, bay leaf, and herb sprigs, reduce the heat to a gentle simmer, and cook until the beans are tender, 35 to 40 minutes (or longer if the beans are old). Just before the beans are done, season with salt to taste.

Reserve ½ cup of the cooking liquid and drain the beans. Remove the vegetables and spread them on a platter or baking sheet to cool slightly. Transfer the beans and garlic to a medium bowl (discard the bay leaf and herb sprigs).

Chop the vegetables into ¼-inch pieces and add to the beans. Add ¼ cup of the reserved cooking liquid, then add the oil, stirring gently. Add some or all of the remaining reserved cooking liquid if the beans seem dry, sprinkle with the chopped thyme, and season with salt and pepper. Serve warm or at room temperature. *(The beans can be refrigerated for up to 3 days; bring to room temperature before serving.)*

Broiled Pumpkin with Apples

SERVES 6 · PHOTO PAGE 45

1 cup apple cider

2 pounds butternut squash, peeled, cut lengthwise in half, seeded, and cut into ½-inch pieces

2 medium Granny Smith apples, peeled, quartered, cored, and cut into ½-inch pieces

3 tablespoons extra virgin olive oil

Maldon or other flaky sea salt and coarsely ground black pepper

2 tablespoons Asian fish sauce

2 tablespoons sherry vinegar

2 tablespoons finely chopped fresh sage

Preheat the broiler. Toss the squash with 2 tablespoons of the oil in a large bowl and season with salt and pepper. Spread the squash out on a baking sheet in a single layer (set the bowl aside) and broil, stirring occasionally, until lightly charred in spots and beginning to soften, about 10 minutes. Toss the apples with the remaining 1 tablespoon oil and season with salt and pepper. Toss with the squash on the baking sheet and cook, stirring occasionally, until the squash and apples are tender. Return to the bowl.

Meanwhile, bring the cider to a boil in a small saucepan and boil until it is syrupy and reduced to 2 tablespoons. Remove from the heat.

Combine the reduced cider, fish sauce, vinegar, and sage in a small bowl and whisk well. Pour over the squash and apples, tossing to coat. Serve, or let stand at room temperature for 1 hour to bring out the flavors. *(The squash and apples can be refrigerated for up to 3 days; bring to room temperature before serving.)*

52

Salsify

WITH BLOOD ORANGE
CITRONETTE

RECIPE PAGE 58

53

Braised Cardoons

WITH BAGNA CAUDA

RECIPE PAGE 59

54
**Black Kale
with Ricotta**
RECIPE PAGE 60

55

Sunchokes with Walnut Gremolata

RECIPE PAGE 60

56

Beets with Pistachios

RECIPE PAGE 62

57

Turnips Braised in Chianti

RECIPE PAGE 63

Salsify with Blood Orange Citronette

SERVES 6 · PHOTO PAGE 52

1 lemon, halved

1½ pounds salsify

3 tablespoons extra virgin olive oil, or as needed

1 cup fresh blood orange juice (or 1 cup regular orange juice plus 1 tablespoon grenadine)

1 tablespoon champagne vinegar

Maldon or other flaky sea salt and coarsely ground black pepper

Fill a medium bowl with water and squeeze the juice of the lemon into it. Peel the salsify and cut it into 2-inch pieces, dropping it into the bowl of water as you go, to prevent oxidation. Just before cooking, drain and pat dry.

Heat 2 tablespoons of the olive oil in a 12-inch sauté pan over medium-high heat. Add half of the salsify and sauté until lightly browned and crisp-tender, 7 to 9 minutes. Transfer to a medium bowl and cook the remaining salsify, adding more oil to the pan if necessary.

Bring the orange juice (and the grenadine, if using) to a boil in a small saucepan and boil until reduced to about 2 tablespoons. Remove from the heat and add the vinegar, the remaining 1 tablespoon oil, and salt and pepper to taste. Pour over the salsify, tossing to mix well. Let cool.

Serve the salsify, or let stand at room temperature for 1 hour longer to bring out the flavors. *(The salsify can be refrigerated for up to 3 days; bring to room temperature before serving.)*

Braised Cardoons with Bagna Cauda

SERVES 6 · PHOTO PAGE 53

2 pounds cardoons

1 cup water

1 cup milk

1 cup dry white wine

¼ cup extra virgin olive oil

Juice of 2 lemons

5 bay leaves, preferably fresh

½ teaspoon peppercorns

1 tablespoon kosher salt

Bagna Cauda (recipe follows)

Cut off the tough bottoms of the cardoons and trim the tops; cut off any leaves. Peel the stalks with a vegetable peeler to remove the fibrous strings. Cut into 3-inch lengths.

Combine the water, milk, wine, olive oil, lemon juice, bay leaves, peppercorns, and salt in a medium pot, add the cardoons, and bring to a gentle simmer. Cover, reduce the heat to very low, and cook until the cardoons are tender, about 40 minutes. Drain.

Serve the cardoons warm or chilled, with the bagna cauda.

BAGNA CAUDA

MAKES ABOUT 1 CUP

¼ cup milk

6 garlic cloves, sliced paper-thin

¾ cup extra virgin olive oil

4 tablespoons unsalted butter

2 tablespoons coarsely chopped anchovy fillets

Coarsely ground black pepper

Combine the milk and garlic in a very small saucepan and bring to a boil over medium heat, then lower the heat and simmer gently for 10 minutes. Drain the garlic, reserving the milk.

Combine the olive oil and butter in a small saucepan and heat over medium heat until the butter is melted. Add the garlic, 1 tablespoon of the reserved milk, the anchovies, and pepper to taste, and remove from the heat. Using an immersion blender, blend until well combined; or transfer to a regular blender and blend well. Serve immediately. *(The sauce will not remain emulsified for very long—that would not be very Italian.)*

Note: Cardoons look like giant celery stalks, but they taste more like artichokes— their cousins. Look for them in Italian or specialty markets in late spring through winter.

Black Kale with Ricotta

SERVES 6 · PHOTO PAGE 54

1½ pounds cavolo nero (also called lacinato or Tuscan kale) or regular kale

6 tablespoons extra virgin olive oil

6 garlic cloves, thickly sliced

1 red finger chile or serrano chile, thinly sliced

Maldon or other flaky sea salt

¾ cup fresh ricotta

Trim the kale, removing the tough stems and ribs, and coarsely chop it.

Combine 2 tablespoons of the oil, the garlic, and chile in a large pot, add the kale, and sauté over medium-high heat for about 5 minutes, until it is beginning to wilt. Season with salt, add ¾ cup water, cover, and cook until the kale is tender, 15 to 20 minutes. Drain and let cool slightly.

Meanwhile, put the ricotta in a small bowl and whisk in the remaining ¼ cup oil. If necessary, whisk in up to 2 tablespoons warm water to loosen the consistency.

Spread the ricotta on a serving plate, spoon the kale over it, and serve.

Sunchokes with Walnut Gremolata

SERVES 6 · PHOTO PAGE 55

¼ cup walnuts, toasted (see page 261) and finely chopped

⅓ cup coarsely chopped fresh Italian parsley

2 tablespoons slivered orange zest

2 garlic cloves, finely chopped

1 pound firm sunchokes (Jerusalem artichokes), scrubbed

2 tablespoons extra virgin olive oil

Maldon or other flaky sea salt and coarsely ground black pepper

Combine the walnuts, parsley, orange zest, and garlic in a small bowl, mixing well.

Using a Benriner (Japanese mandoline) or other vegetable slicer, thinly shave the sunchokes. Transfer to a bowl and drizzle with the olive oil, tossing well (be sure to coat the sunchokes well, to prevent oxidation). Season with salt and pepper, sprinkle with the gremolata, and serve.

Beets with Pistachios

SERVES 6 · PHOTO PAGE 56

2 large bunches medium beets, preferably
a combination of red and golden beets,
trimmed (not peeled) and scrubbed

1 tablespoon olive oil

Kosher salt

½ cup shelled pistachios, preferably Sicilian,
plus (optional) chopped pistachios for
garnish

About ¼ cup warm water

2 tablespoons pistachio oil

2 tablespoons Red Wine Vinaigrette
(page 23)

Maldon or other flaky sea salt and coarsely
ground black pepper

Preheat the oven to 400°F.

Toss the beets with the olive oil and a
light sprinkling of kosher salt in a medium
bowl. Spread the beets out in a baking pan
and roast until tender, 50 to 60 minutes.
Remove from the oven and let cool slightly.

Meanwhile, pulse the pistachios in a food
processor until fairly finely ground. Add 3
tablespoons water and pulse to incorporate
it. Add the oil and pulse until smooth, adding up to 1½ more tablespoons water if
necessary. *(The pistachio butter can be made
ahead and refrigerated for up to 3 days; bring
to room temperature before serving.)*

Rub the skins off the beets with a paper
towel. Cut into 1-inch chunks and transfer
to a serving bowl. Toss the beets with the
vinaigrette and let stand for at least 10
minutes, or for up to 1 hour, before serving.
*(The beets can refrigerated for up to 3 days;
bring to room temperature before serving.)*

Transfer the beets to a platter or plates
and sprinkle with the remaining pistachios.
Spoon the pistachio butter alongside and
serve.

Turnips Braised in Chianti

SERVES 6 · PHOTO PAGE 57

2 pounds medium turnips, trimmed (a few greens reserved for garnish if desired), peeled, and cut into 8 wedges each

About 2 cups Chianti or other dry red wine

¼ cup honey

¼ cup Red Wine Vinaigrette (page 23)

Maldon or other flaky sea salt and coarsely ground black pepper

Combine the turnips and wine to cover in a medium pot and bring to a boil over medium-high heat. Reduce the heat to a low boil, cover, and cook until the turnips are just tender, about 40 minutes.

Drain the turnips, reserving the cooking liquid, and transfer to a bowl. Pour the liquid back into the pot, bring to a boil, and boil until reduced to a syrupy glaze, 7 to 10 minutes. Remove from the heat and stir in the honey.

Add the glaze and vinaigrette to the turnips, stirring to mix well, and season with salt and pepper. Serve, or let stand at room temperature for 1 hour to bring out the flavors. *(The turnips can be refrigerated for up to 3 days; bring to room temperature before serving.)*

SEAFOOD & MEAT ANTIPASTI

I've spent a lot of time

developing a cured-meat ideology, and I credit my dad and family in Seattle for really taking it to the next level at Salumi Artisan Cured Meats. Check out their stuff at www.salumicuredmeats.com—it is truly remarkable. We are not including recipes for making your own cured meats in this book, as making them at home as an amateur is now deemed risky by health departments across this great land, but I know that many of you will continue to do so, and I wish you great success. On page 79, you will find a list of my faves that we make at Otto, along with other excellent options as to where and how to procure the best stuff. And keep in mind that while it seems often quite expensive when you look at the per-pound price, for a group of 6 or 8 people, a half pound of two or three things is plenty if served in conjunction with a couple of the antipasti from this book, and then a pasta or pizza or two afterward.

Because I grew up in Seattle, seafood has a special place in my heart. The five seafood antipasti recipes in this chapter, some of our favorites that we serve at Otto, are simple to make and easy to shop for. Seafood can be tricky, as its shelf life is much briefer than that of most of the other ingredients in this book. The easiest way to do it is to make sure your guests are as piscatorially interested as you are. None of the ingredients called for are very expensive, except for the tuna—which will, in fact, keep for almost a week when cooked and preserved this way.

68

Mussels with Peperonata

RECIPE PAGE 74

69

Anchovies with Fried Bread

RECIPE PAGE 75

70

Octopus & Celery

RECIPE PAGE 76

71

Sardines in Saor

RECIPE PAGE 77

72

Preserved Tuna

RECIPE OPPOSITE

Seafood Antipasti

Preserved Tuna

SERVES 6 · PHOTO PAGE OPPOSITE

1 pound tuna belly, rinsed and patted dry, skin and any tough membrane removed, trimmed of any dark spots, and cut into 1-inch cubes

1 tablespoon celery seeds

1 tablespoon fennel seeds

1 tablespoon Maldon or other flaky sea salt, plus more for garnish

1 tablespoon sugar

About 1 cup extra virgin olive oil

¼ cup finely chopped fresh Italian parsley

Grated zest and juice of 1 lemon, or to taste

Put the tuna cubes in a small baking dish that holds them in a single layer. Combine the celery seeds, fennel seeds, salt, and sugar in a small bowl, mixing well. Sprinkle generously over the tuna, turning to coat on all sides. Let stand for 20 minutes.

Preheat the oven to 250°F.

Pour the oil over the tuna; it should just cover it. Cover the baking dish tightly with plastic wrap (it will not melt in a 250°F oven). Put the dish in the oven and cook for 20 to 25 minutes, until the tuna is just cooked through—cut into a piece to test: it should no longer be pink (an instant-read thermometer should read 110°F). Remove from the oven and let cool in the oil. *(The tuna can be refrigerated in the oil for up to 5 days.)*

To serve, drain the tuna and transfer to a serving dish or plate. Sprinkle with the parsley and lemon zest, drizzle with the lemon juice, and sprinkle with salt.

Mussels with Peperonata

SERVES 6 · PHOTO PAGE 68

5 garlic cloves, thinly sliced

½ cup extra virgin olive oil

1 pound red bell peppers (3 large), cored, seeded, and cut into ½-inch dice

1 pound green bell peppers (3 large), cored, seeded, and cut into ½-inch dice

1 red finger chile or serrano chile, thinly sliced

¾ cup dry white wine

2 pounds PEI or other small mussels, scrubbed and debearded

1 cup Pomì strained tomatoes, simmered until reduced by half

3 tablespoons salt-packed capers, rinsed and soaked overnight in cold water (change the water often)

Maldon or other flaky sea salt

Combine half the garlic and ¼ cup of the oil in a 12-inch sauté pan and heat over medium-low heat just until the garlic is slightly softened, about 1 minute; do not allow to color. Add the bell peppers and sliced chile and cook, stirring occasionally, until the peppers are softened, 15 to 20 minutes. Transfer to a medium bowl and let cool.

Combine the remaining ¼ cup oil and the remaining garlic in a large pot and cook, stirring, over medium-high heat just until the garlic is slightly softened, about 1 minute. Add the wine and mussels, cover, and steam until the mussels open, about 4 minutes; transfer the mussels to a bowl as they open. Remove the pot from the heat and set aside.

Add the tomato sauce, capers, and pepper mixture to the mussel broth and bring to a simmer. Season with salt to taste, remove from the heat, and gently stir in the mussels. Serve warm or at room temperature. *(The mussels can be refrigerated for up to 3 days; serve cold, or bring to room temperature before serving.)*

Anchovies with Fried Bread

SERVES 6 · PHOTO PAGE 69

Four ½-inch-thick slices filone or other
  crusty bread, cut into ½-inch cubes

About ¼ cup extra virgin olive oil

4 ounces marinated white anchovies
  (boquerones), drained, any liquid reserved

4 scallions, thinly sliced

Preheat the oven to 350°F.

Toss the bread with 2 tablespoons of the oil
and spread out in a single layer on a baking
sheet. Toast in the oven until dark golden
brown, about 12 minutes.

Combine the anchovies, croutons, and scallions in a medium bowl, tossing to mix.
Whisk the reserved anchovy liquid, then
add enough olive oil to make 2 tablespoons.
Add to the anchovies, stirring gently. Let
stand at room temperature for at least
2 hours before serving. *(The anchovies can
be refrigerated for up to 3 days; bring to room
temperature before serving.)*

Octopus & Celery

SERVES 6 · PHOTO PAGE 70

One 3-pound octopus (frozen is fine), sac, beak, and eyes removed (have the fishmonger do this)

1½ cups dry white wine

2 small red onions, thinly sliced

2 carrots, thinly sliced

2 celery ribs, thinly sliced

3 garlic cloves, smashed and peeled

1 bay leaf, preferably fresh

1 sprig each fresh Italian parsley, sage, rosemary, and thyme

1 celery heart with tender leaves, base cut off, fibrous strings removed with a vegetable peeler, and thinly sliced

¼ cup red wine vinegar

¼ cup extra virgin olive oil

Maldon or other flaky sea salt

Combine the octopus, wine, onions, carrots, sliced celery ribs, herbs, and a wine cork, if you have one (the cork helps tenderize the octopus), in a large pot, add enough water to cover the octopus, and bring to boil over high heat. Reduce the heat to medium, cover, and simmer gently until the thickest part of the octopus is tender when pierced with a knife, about 1 hour. Remove from the heat and allow to cool in the broth.

Drain the octopus (discard the vegetables and cork). Cut off the tentacles and strip the skin and suckers from the tentacles (the skin will come off easily once the octopus is cooked). Cut the head and tentacles into 1-inch pieces.

Combine the octopus, sliced celery heart, vinegar, and oil in a large bowl, mixing well. Season well with salt and serve, or let stand for 1 hour to bring out the flavors. *(The octopus can be refrigerated for up to 3 days; bring to room temperature before serving.)*

Sardines in Saor

SERVES 6 · PHOTO PAGE 71

1 medium fennel bulb

1 pound fresh sardines

Maldon or other flaky sea salt

½ cup champagne vinegar

2 tablespoons sugar

1 bay leaf, preferably fresh

1 teaspoon ground cinnamon

¼ cup raisins

¼ cup pine nuts, toasted (see page 261)

Cut the stalks off the fennel bulb and reserve the fronds for garnish. Halve the fennel bulb lengthwise. Using a Benriner (Japanese mandoline) or other vegetable slicer, shave the fennel into paper-thin slices; or use a large sharp knife to slice it as thin as possible.

To prepare the sardines, scrape off any scales with a blunt knife; cut off the fins. Cut off the head and tail of each fish and slit it open down the stomach. Pull out the backbone and the guts (a messy job but quite easy). Open out the fish and cut the 2 fillets apart. Rinse the sardines well under cold water to remove any blood, and pat dry.

Lay the fillets skin side up in a baking dish that holds them in a single layer, sprinkle with salt, and scatter the shaved fennel over them.

Combine the vinegar, sugar, bay leaf, cinnamon, and raisins in a small saucepan, bring to a boil, stirring to dissolve the sugar, and boil for 3 minutes. Pour the vinegar mixture evenly over the sardines. Let cool before serving. *(The sardines can be refrigerated for up to 3 days; serve cold, or bring to room temperature before serving.)*

Just before serving, scatter the pine nuts and reserved fennel fronds over the sardines.

PROSCIUTTO
LA QUERCIA

PROSCIUTTO
DI PARMA

PROSCIUTTO
DI SAN DANIELE

Meat Antipasti

These are the delectable salumi we serve as antipasti. It's best to choose several different types to create a varied platter. I like a spiced salami as the core of the plate, along with a whole muscle like coppa or prosciutto and a fatter one like lardo or pancetta.

PROSCIUTTO CRUDO DOLCE is the general term for an air-dried salt-cured ham made from pigs that weigh in at around 350 pounds. The hams are generally hung, after a traditional salting process, for at least 300 days, often for up to 24 or 36 months. The apparent appreciation for jamón Jabugo de Bellota, also called jamón ibérico, in Spain and now in the world "luxury goods market" has Italian prosciutto makers rethinking the potential for flavor development, and older and older hams will be on the market from each of the following as this new style develops. The best way to understand the differences is to go to a place that allows and promotes sampling and taste your options. Then go with what you love—simple and easy.

These three varieties are our favorites: **PROSCIUTTO DI PARMA** is from Emilia-Romagna's Langhirano, between the Taro and the Baganza Rivers, near Parma. This ham is the king. The pigs are often fed the whey left from Parmigiano-Reggiano production, and we love the 18-month versions made by Galoni and Greci e Folzani. **PROSCIUTTO DI SAN DANIELE** is slightly sweeter than the Parma hams, in our opinion—because of the cooler ambient temperatures, a little less salt is used. These come from the San Daniele and Sauris regions of Friuli, and we love Fratelli Beretta and Principe. **PROSCIUTTO LA QUERCIA**, made by our friends Herb and Kathy Eckhouse in Iowa, is the best American prosciutto on the market. It is fragrant and more pork roasty than either of the Italian versions above. We love both their Green Label and their Rossa; their website is www.laquercia.us.

There are also hams called **PROSCIUTTI CRUDI SALATI** produced throughout regions farther south in Italy, including Toscana, Umbria, and Le Marche. These are more heavily salted and often have pepper and herbs such as rosemary or bay leaves and garlic.

Perhaps the most royal of all ham products is **CULATELLO**, made in the Bassa Parmense and Bassa Verdiana regions near Zibello in northern Emilia-Romagna. It was developed in these higher-humidity, lower-altitude regions as an alternative to prosciutto, and it comes from the largest muscle area at the top of the same rear thighs used to make prosciutto. Culatello is salted and often marinated in wine, then stuffed into a pig's bladder and tied before being hung in these humid conditions. It is not legal for import into the U.S., but Salumi in Seattle makes the best one in the States, and we make a pretty mean one at Babbo as well. Otherwise, your best bet is to eat lots of culatello when you visit Italy, where slices are often served with the odd pat of butter and the strange cracker-like bread of northern Emilia.

We make all of the products below under the careful and fully HAACP-certified program developed by chef Dan Drohan at Otto and in part by chef Zach Allen, now at Carnevino in Las Vegas.

COPPA, often called "the poor man's prosciutto," is made from the muscles at the top of the shoulder near the base of the neck. The D.O.C. product from Italy is from Piacenza; it is traditionally cured with cookie spices such as cinnamon, cloves, and nutmeg, along with salt and pepper, that are all massaged in, and then the whole fandango is packed into a beef bung and hung for 120 days. The one we make at Otto has cayenne and fennel seeds too.

BRESAOLA is air-dried beef eye of round, traditionally from the Valtellina in Lombardia. We rub ours with salt and pepper and a little sugar, bag it in beef bungs like the coppa, and hang it for 70 days. In Italy, bresaola is often served with sliced raw artichokes as an antipasto, or with robiola cheese.

LONZA is made from boneless pork loin, where pork chops come from. We cure ours with salt and fennel and hang it, unsheathed but tied like a roast, for 90 days.

PANCETTA is pork belly cured whole, like slab bacon, with sugar, bay, cinnamon, black pepper, and allspice. It is hung for 70 days, then either rolled (*rotolata*) or left flat (*stesa*). It is eaten raw, sliced thinly like prosciutto, or cooked like bacon.

LARDO is made from the fatback of pigs that weigh in at up to 500 pounds, to produce very thick and succulent, very fragrant and creamy lard. The D.O.P. version comes from Colonnata in the Apuan Alps of northern Toscana, where it is aged in marble-veined caves originally excavated for use in sculptures. We pack ours tightly in a wet "sand" of salt, pepper, ginger, rosemary, and allspice and let it rest, unexposed to light, for 6 to 8 months, then hang it for 60 to 120 days more before slicing it and serving it on hot bruschetta or pizza bianca.

GUANCIALE is made from the entire jowl and cheek of a large pig. We rub ours with marjoram, black and red pepper, and brown sugar and let it rest, away from light, for 42 days, then hang it for 30 days. We cook it or slice it and serve it raw. Guanciale is the base fat for much of Roman and Abruzzese cooking, especially pastas and many vegetable dishes.

GUANCIALE

PANCETTA

LARDO

BRESAOLA

SALAMI
LARDETTO

SALAMI WITH
CELERY

PEPPERONI

COPPA

LONZA

FINOCCHIONA

FINOCCHIONA, originally from Toscana, is flavored with fennel seeds and an aggressive amount of salt and black pepper. At Otto, we add ground coriander and cayenne, stuff it into hog middles, and hang it for 45 days before slicing and serving it while it is still relatively soft.

PEPPERONI is the classic spicy salami known and appreciated by pizza lovers all over the world. We make ours with cayenne, red pepper flakes, a touch of vinegar, and fennel pollen and dry it for 60 days to achieve the customary firm texture that cooks up perfectly on a tomato and mozzarella pie.

SALAMI TOSCANO could actually be anything made by a butcher in Toscana, but it usually has whole black peppercorns, wine, and some form of fennel in a base of quite coarsely ground pork and fat. We hang ours for 90 days for a firm texture; a lot of butchers in Toscana hang it for much less, depending on local custom. We use a lactic starter to achieve the traditional flavor in this and the salami lardetto. **SALAMI LARDETTO**, which has much larger pieces of hand-cut cubed fat, not ground, is what many Italians consider salami toscana. We use pieces of cured lardo as well to tune up the intensity. **SALAMI WITH CELERY** is a variation on the toscano, with the addition of celery seeds and a touch of corn syrup solids for a pungent celery punch and a slightly sweeter mouthfeel. It is one of my all-time faves.

TESTA is an Italian head cheese. We brine a whole hog's head with brown sugar, salt, bay leaf, and garlic for 3 days and then poach it with oranges and peppercorns. We remove all of the meat from the bones, add a little natural gelatin to some of the poaching liquid, and set the entire beautiful mess in cylindrical bain-maries to achieve the classic shape. We serve it sliced a bit thicker than traditional salami. In Panzano, in Toscana, our favorite Italian butcher in the world and pal Dario Cecchini makes something like this as big as a torpedo and calls it soppressata. To eat it served from his hands is one of the seven gastronomic wonders of the world and well worth a trip to Italy by itself.

MORTADELLA was born in Bologna, Emilia-Romagna, and that is where our word for bologna the lunch meat got its name. In Italy, mortadella is considered one of the pinnacles of Emilian gastronomy, and it can be the defining point of a good party when served with proper abandon, sometimes with freshly grated horseradish and mustard. I am a big fan of a dry mortadella panino served with a tiny cold beer around 10 a.m. for a little breaky break when I am in Bologna—or Venezia, for that matter. It is essentially a smooth paste of finely ground and highly seasoned pork, often studded with cubes of fat and pistachios. It is always cooked, either in large steam ovens or poached slowly in giant vessels; it does not need aging.

BRUSCHETTA & CHEESE

For many Italian kids

at university these days, bruschetta is the new pizza and it can be thought of in the same way in terms of toppings, from simple to complex. Although the word *bruschetta* comes from the Roman dialectical verb root *bruscare* (which means "to cook or roast over hot coals"), we use an industrial toaster at Otto, and you can use a simple toaster oven, a panino press, or a regular oven broiler for equally delicious results. One tip is to cook the bread a little bit longer than you think—a deep dark golden brown crust yields a much more complex flavor, and the crunch is indispensable for a great bruschetta experience.

As a simple and delicious way to turn a couple of bruschette into a nice light meal, serving a few well-chosen cheeses can also be a fun way to explore regional variations in the key of milk. Often served at the end of the meal, cheese has really become its own category at both simple and fancy enotecas in all of my favorite towns throughout Italy.

86

Artichokes

RECIPE PAGE 90

87

Tomato & Lardo

RECIPES PAGE 91

88

Cabbage

RECIPE OPPOSITE

Bruschetta

MAKES 6 TOASTS

Six ¾-inch-thick slices filone or other
country bread

2 garlic cloves, peeled

Grill or toast the bread, turning once, until
marked with grill marks or deep golden
brown but still soft in the center. Rub a
garlic clove just around the circumference
of each toast, along the jagged outer crust.
Divide the topping of your choice among
the bruschetta, and serve.

**Each of the following topping recipes
makes enough for 6 bruschetta, to
serve 6.**

WHITE BEANS

SERVES 6

Use ½ recipe (a generous 2 cups) White
Beans (page 50).

CABBAGE

**MAKES A GENEROUS 2 CUPS
PHOTO OPPOSITE**

2 tablespoons extra virgin olive oil

2 tablespoons unsalted butter

2 ounces smoked bacon, cut into ¼-inch dice

½ medium white onion, thinly sliced

1 pound red or white cabbage (about
½ medium cabbage), halved, cored, and
cut crosswise into ½-inch-wide ribbons

2 tablespoons red wine vinegar

Maldon or other flaky sea salt and coarsely
ground black pepper

Combine the oil, butter, bacon, onion, and
cabbage in a large pot and cook over medium-high heat, stirring, until the cabbage is
well coated and beginning to wilt, about
5 minutes. Cover, reduce the heat to low,
and cook until the cabbage is very tender,
20 to 25 minutes.

Add the vinegar, increase the heat to high,
and cook, stirring, until most of the cooking liquid has evaporated. Season with salt
if necessary and with pepper and remove
from the heat.

Serve the cabbage warm or at room temperature. *(The cabbage can be refrigerated for
up to 3 days; bring to room temperature before
serving.)*

ARTICHOKES

MAKES A GENEROUS 2 CUPS · PHOTO PAGE 86

3 cups water

1 cup dry white wine

Juice of 2 lemons

1 pound baby artichokes (10 to 12)

¼ cup coarsely chopped fresh basil, stems reserved

½ large white onion, cut into ¼-inch dice

5 garlic cloves, smashed and peeled

1 bay leaf, preferably fresh

¼ cup extra virgin olive oil

Maldon or other flaky sea salt

Combine the water, wine, and lemon juice in a medium bowl. Pull off the tough outer leaves from each artichoke, then cut off the top ½ inch of the remaining leaves. Trim the bottom of the artichoke stem, then cut off the top outer layer of the stem with a paring knife. Transfer the artichokes to the lemon juice mixture as you work, to prevent oxidation.

Transfer the artichokes and their liquid to a medium pot. Add the basil stems, onion, garlic, and bay leaf, put a pan lid on top of the artichokes to keep them submerged, and bring to a boil. Reduce the heat to a simmer and cook until the artichokes are tender (test the centers with the tip of a sharp knife), 10 to 15 minutes. Drain, reserving the onion and garlic, and let cool slightly; discard the basil stems and bay leaf.

Quarter each artichoke with a sharp knife (remove and discard any remaining tough leaves if necessary). Chop or mash the garlic.

Transfer the artichokes, onion, and garlic to a sauté pan, add the oil, and cook over medium heat, stirring occasionally, until all the artichoke leaves are tender, 12 to 15 minutes. Season with salt, stir in the chopped basil, and remove from the heat.

Serve the artichokes warm or at room temperature. *(The artichokes can be refrigerated for up to 3 days; bring to room temperature before serving.)*

TOMATO

SERVES 6 · PHOTO PAGE 87

3 large ripe tomatoes, such as Brandywine, beefsteak, or Jersey

2 tablespoons extra virgin olive oil

Maldon or other flaky sea salt

Cut the tomatoes in half. Rub the toasted bruschetta with the cut sides of the tomato halves, squeezing the tomatoes so that the bread absorbs the juice and is coated with the pulp and seeds. Drizzle with the olive oil, sprinkle with salt, and serve.

LARDO

SERVES 6 · PHOTO PAGE 87

2 ounces lardo (cured fatback), preferably from Salumi Artisan Cured Meats (see Sources, page 266), chilled and very thinly sliced

Maldon or other flaky sea salt and coarsely ground black pepper

Arrange the slices of lardo on the bruschetta and sprinkle with salt and pepper.

BROCCOLI RABE

MAKES ABOUT 1½ CUPS

¼ cup extra virgin olive oil

5 garlic cloves, thinly sliced

8 ounces broccoli rabe, trimmed

Maldon or other flaky sea salt

½ teaspoon hot red pepper flakes

A 4-ounce chunk of ricotta salata for grating

Combine 2 tablespoons of the olive oil and the garlic in a large pot and cook, stirring, over medium-high heat until the garlic is fragrant, about 1 minute. Add the broccoli rabe and cook, stirring and tossing, until beginning to wilt, 2 to 3 minutes. Add ½ cup water, cover, reduce the heat to low, and cook, stirring occasionally, until the broccoli rabe is very soft, about 20 minutes. Drain if necessary, and transfer to a bowl.

Season the broccoli rabe with salt to taste and the red pepper flakes, and toss with the remaining 2 tablespoons oil. Serve warm or at room temperature. *(The broccoli rabe can be refrigerated for up to 3 days; bring to room temperature before serving.)*

Arrange the broccoli rabe on top of the bruschetta and grate some cheese over each one.

CECI

MAKES ABOUT 1¾ CUPS · PHOTO PAGE 84

2 tablespoons extra virgin olive oil, plus extra for drizzling

½ large red onion, halved lengthwise and thinly sliced

Maldon or other flaky sea salt

Hot red pepper flakes

One 15-ounce can chickpeas, rinsed and drained

Heat the oil in a large pot over medium heat. Add the onion, season with salt and red pepper flakes, and cook, stirring occasionally, until the onion is beginning to soften, about 5 minutes. Add the chickpeas, reduce the heat to medium-low, and cook, stirring occasionally, for 5 minutes to blend the flavors. Season with additional salt and/or red pepper flakes if necessary and serve warm or at room temperature. *(The chickpeas can be refrigerated for up to 3 days; bring to room temperature before serving.)*

Divide the chickpeas among the bruschetta, mashing the chickpeas with a fork as you do so. Drizzle with olive oil and serve.

ONION RAGU

MAKES ABOUT 1⅔ CUPS

¼ cup extra virgin olive oil

1 pound sweet onions, such as Vidalia or Walla Walla, or Bermuda onions, thinly sliced

5 garlic cloves, thinly sliced

Maldon or other flaky sea salt and coarsely ground black pepper

Combine the olive oil, onions, and garlic in a large pot, season with salt and pepper, and cook over medium heat, stirring occasionally, until the onions are beginning to soften, 5 to 7 minutes. Add ⅓ cup water, cover, reduce the heat to low, and cook, stirring occasionally, until the onions are very soft, 15 to 20 minutes. If necessary, increase the heat to high and cook uncovered, stirring occasionally, until most of the cooking liquid has evaporated.

Taste the onions and add additional salt and/or pepper if necessary. Remove from the heat and serve warm or at room temperature. *(The onions can be refrigerated for up to 3 days; bring to room temperature before serving.)*

LEEK RAGU

MAKES ABOUT 1 CUP

¼ cup extra virgin olive oil

5 garlic cloves, coarsely chopped

1 pound leeks, trimmed, halved lengthwise, cut into ½-inch-thick slices, and washed well

Maldon or other flaky sea salt and coarsely ground black pepper

Heat the oil in a large pot over medium heat. Add the garlic and cook, stirring, until soft, 1 to 2 minutes. Add the leeks, season with salt and pepper, and cook, stirring, until softened but not browned, 8 to 10 minutes. Add ⅓ cup water, cover, reduce the heat to low, and cook gently until the leeks are very soft, about 15 minutes. If necessary, increase the heat to high and cook uncovered, stirring occasionally, until most of the cooking liquid has evaporated.

Taste the leeks and add additional salt and/or pepper if necessary. Remove from the heat and serve warm or at room temperature. *(The leeks can be refrigerated for up to 3 days; bring to room temperature before serving.)*

EGGPLANT

MAKES ABOUT 2 CUPS

1 pound.eggplant, cut into 1-inch cubes

Kosher salt

¼ cup extra virgin olive oil

¾ cup Pomì strained tomatoes

2 tablespoons coarsely chopped fresh mint

½ teaspoon hot red pepper flakes

Put the eggplant in a colander set on a plate, sprinkle generously with salt, and let stand for 20 minutes.

Preheat the broiler. Rinse the eggplant, drain, and pat dry. Toss with 2 tablespoons of the oil and spread on a baking sheet. Broil, stirring and turning the eggplant occasionally, until it is charred in spots and just tender, 15 to 20 minutes. Transfer to a bowl.

Meanwhile, bring the tomato sauce to a boil in a small saucepan and boil, stirring occasionally, until as thick as ketchup. Stir in the mint and red pepper flakes.

Add the tomato mixture to the eggplant, stirring well. Stir in the remaining 2 tablespoons oil and serve warm or at room temperature. *(The eggplant can be refrigerated for up to 3 days; bring to room temperature before serving.)*

MARZOLINO

BAITA
FRIULI

10

PARMIGIANO-
REGGIANO

BRA
TENERO

SAMPIETRINO

VENTO
D'ESTATE

UBRIACO

CASTEL ROSSO

TUADA

CACIOTTA

PECORINO
ROMANO

Cheese

At Otto, the centerpiece of the antipasto station is the cheese. The arrangement is simple but important—and when serving cheese at home, the presentation helps lead your guests' mind a bit. So always arrange the cheeses you are serving with a little style on a tray, or even on a board on your kitchen counter.

We serve apricot mostarda and black truffle honey with our cheese plates (see page 103). Other cheese condiments we love include amarena cherries (see Sources, page 266), *membrillo* (quince paste), pomegranate molasses, pear chutney, fig jam . . . the list goes on.

PARMIGIANO-REGGIANO is the undisputed king of cheeses, and its production is strictly regulated under D.O.C. laws: the cheese must have been made entirely in a restricted area that includes only the provinces of Parma, Modena, and Reggio-Emilia and parts of Bologna and Mantova. The rind of true Parmigiano is always imprinted all over with the term "Parmigiano-Reggiano," verifying its authenticity. Some Parmigiano enthusiasts claim to prefer cheeses made in the late spring and summer months, when the animals' feed is fresh grass and wheat.

I like all of them, but I do prefer a younger cheese for eating unadorned or with balsamic vinegar and an older cheese for grating over my pasta and risotto.

PECORINO ROMANO, the familiar firm sheep's-milk cheese, is named for the original Romans who made and ate so much of it, but today it is produced not necessarily in or near Rome—it is now made in Maremma, Sardegna, parts of Abruzzo, and in Lazio. When young and recently opened, pecorino romano is an excellent table cheese, often paired with fresh pears or figs. When aged, its saltiness makes it almost exclusively a grating cheese. It is indispensable in pasta dishes such as bucatini all'amatriciana and rigatoni cacio e pepe, but it is also excellent as the saline component in many vegetable dishes, especially when paired with guanciale as the cooking fat.

PECORINO DI FOSSA, an aged sheep's-milk cheese produced in Emilia-Romagna and Le Marche, has a rich, earthy flavor. Often wrapped in the leaves of chestnut or walnut trees, the cheese is aged in caves *(fosse)* for a minimum of 3 months. It is tradition-

CACIO DI ROMA

BEL PAESE

COACH FARM
TRIPLE CREAM

BLU DI
LANGA

COACH FARM
GREEN PEPPERCORN
BRICK

SMOKED RICOTTA

MOZZARELLA
DI BUFALA

ally unearthed and celebrated on the Feast of Santa Caterina in late November. It is most often grated over pasta, but it can also be enjoyed on its own. I love it with its soulmate, black truffles, served in the form of honey (see page 103).

TUADA is an unusual Tuscan pecorino, in that we cannot be sure from the label if there is not a touch of cow's milk along with the sheep's milk in it as well. Aged for 60 days and thus referred to as "*semi stagionato,*" it is a semi-firm cheese with a nutty flavor, a crazy bubbly curd, and a cement-gray outer surface. It makes a mean salad with fresh hard pears, but it also grates well over a pizza Margherita, in combination with fresh mozzarella, for serious depth of flavor.

VENTO D'ESTATE is a cow's-milk cheese that is aged in nests of freshly mown hay in wine barrels, both of which contribute to its unique flavor and aroma (its name means "summer breeze"). Made near Treviso, in the Veneto, by Antonio Carpendo, it has only been produced since the late 1990s. With a firm but crumbly texture, it has a rich, somewhat sharp taste and goes well with a robust red wine.

CACIOTTA cheeses, which may be made with ewe's and/or cow's milk, are produced in Tuscany, Umbria, and New York State. The American one is made by Jody Sommers from cow's milk, and it is rubbed with tomato paste before it is aged for 100 days. The Tuscan and Umbrian ones are made from a blend of cow's and ewe's milk and are often the vehicles for flavorings such as truffles—go for the plain ones, please.

BAITA FRIULI is an unpasteurized cow's-milk cheese, aged for roughly 5 months, from Italy's Friuli-Venezia region, near the Slovenian border. It has a fruity, slightly spicy flavor similar to that of a good Swiss Gruyère. It can be served as part of a cheese plate or used for cooking, in a fondue or for grating.

BRA cheeses, made with unpasteurized cow's milk, are named for the town of Bra in Italy's Piedmont, but they are not made there—they are actually produced on the Cuneo plains. They are sold either *duro* (firm) or *tenero* (soft or tender), and the **BRA TENERO** we like is semi-soft and mild.

UBRIACO, a cow's-milk cheese from the Veneto, is produced by the same dude who makes Vento d'Estate. It is aged in red wine (*ubriaco* means "drunk"), and it is moist but firm, with a somewhat sweet but sharp and delightfully spicy flavor. Its granular texture is similar to Parmigiano, with an off-the-cuff scent of pineapple.

CASTEL ROSSO, an ancient cow's-milk cheese from Piedmont, is a semi-firm cheese with a crumbly texture and a mild, slightly tangy flavor that whispers mushrooms to me. Smoother in texture and softer under heat than its aged cousin Castel Magno, this champ begs to sing melted on a bruschetta or a pizza bianca.

BURRATA

GORGONZOLA

TALEGGIO

FRESH
RICOTTA

STRACCHINO
DI CRESCENZA

BRUNET

BRUNET

Tomazzetta stagionata di pura capra
Caseificio dell'Alta Langa

BRUNET is a Piemontese fresh goat's-milk cheese with a rich, slightly tangy flavor and a creamy, almost silky, texture. It works very well as a light player on a plate with three or four more intense cheeses.

MOZZARELLA DI BUFALA has more flavor than cow's-milk mozzarella; it is sweet with a slight tang and a creamy, milky bite (although some artisanal producers are now using cow's milk for their mozzarella, with slightly different but very good results). Mozzarella di bufala is available salted or unsalted; it can also be smoked.

JOE'S DAIRY MOZZARELLA, made at 156 Sullivan Street in New York's Soho by our pal Anthony Campanelli, is the epitome of fresh handmade mozzarella in the USA: clean, fresh, and tasting only of milk. We use it on pizzas that need a touch of lactic love but do not need any more moisture, like that exuded by a mozzarella di bufala from Campania. Check out the store for other great snackage as well.

BURRATA, like mozzarella, is a "pulled-curd" cheese, but this cow's-milk (traditionally made with buffalo milk) cheese has a surprise inside: the cheese is shaped into a pouch around a rich, creamy, melting center of mozzarella curds mixed with cream.

STRACCHINO is in fact a family and style of cow's-milk cheeses from Lombardy, also made in the Piemonte and Veneto. The name refers to cattle that are tired (*straco* in dialect, *stanco* in Italian) after the end-of-summer trek down from their mountain-grazing vacations. Sometimes called stracchino di crescenza, or just crescenza, these cheeses have a rich, acidic flavor with a soft, almost runny texture at room temperature. Both Taleggio and Toma Piemontese are stracchino cheeses, each a little more pungent due to the rind-washing and aging strategies involved.

COACH FARM TRIPLE CREAM, an aged goat's-milk cheese from my wife, Susi's, family farm in New York's Hudson Valley, has a rich, almost sweet, buttery flavor that defines what great American cheese making can be. It is an excellent cheese plate choice, and it also does well melted in a pasta like cacio e pepe or in the sophisticated mac-and-cheese of any rich man or woman.

COACH FARM GREEN PEPPERCORN BRICK, also from Susi's family, is a crumbly aged goat's-milk cheese that is studded with green peppercorns. It goes very well with fruit condiments, such as our apricot mostarda.

FRESH RICOTTA is not actually a cheese, but a by-product of the cheese-making process. Its name means "recooked," and it is traditionally made from the whey left over from the day's cheese making, reheated until it forms curds and then drained. Italian ricotta is usually made from whey from sheep's or water buffalo milk; most American ricotta is made from cow's-milk whey. Fresh Italian ricotta has a mild, nutty, sweet flavor and a drier texture than most American ricottas.

SMOKED RICOTTA is a smoked log or "button" of fresh sheep's-milk ricotta from Puglia or Calabria. Ours is made by Caseificio Abbasciano. It has a delicate smoky tang that does not overwhelm the creamy, sheepy flavor and a moist texture reminiscent of wet sand. We like it crumbled over pastas with tomato-based sauces as well as on a cheese board.

MARZOLINO is an exceptional semi-soft young pecorino toscano with a smooth, creamy texture and a mild nutty flavor. This sheep's-milk cheese is released each March, hence the name. Unaged Marzolino is called Raviggiuolo and is rarely shipped, as it is delicate and highly perishable. If you see either one, buy it and eat it at home behind closed doors.

CACIO DI ROMA, a semi-firm sheep's-milk cheese from Lazio, is one of our favorites. It has a smooth texture and a mild flavor, and because it melts well, it is used in many pastas and other dishes, but it can also be served on its own.

BEL PAESE is a soft, creamy, mild cow's-milk cheese invented in the twentieth century to mimic a French melting cheese. True Italian Bel Paese comes from Lombardy. It can be served on a cheese plate or used in cooking, but it works best for me as a second or third cheese on a pizza.

TALEGGIO, a soft-ripened cow's-milk cheese from Lombardy, is a member of the stracchino clan. It has a washed rind that goes from a straw yellow when young and firm to a deep orange when older and runny. With a silky texture and a strong flavor even when young, the fragrant cheese becomes more assertive and tangy as it matures, and when aged perfectly, it can develop crystallized formations in the crust.

BLU DI LANGA is a creamy, mild semi-soft blue cheese from the Piemonte region of Italy. It is made from cow's, sheep's, and goat's milk and has a Brie-like curd marked by pale blue striations.

GORGONZOLA, created outside of Milano in Lombardia, is a blue-veined cow's-milk cheese that is on the level of Parmigiano-Reggiano in terms of greatness. Creamy and rich, with a flavor that goes from powerful and restrained to huge and voluptuous as it ages, it is a perfect cheese to serve instead of dessert when there is still a great wine on the table. We love it with amarene cherries, but it is also perfect with raw autumn fruits and exquisite alone with just crusty bread.

SAMPIETRINO, a cow's- and sheep's-milk blend from Lombardia, is aged for 120 days. The name comes from the shape, which is reminiscent of the cobblestones used to pave Rome. Hard as a rock outside but creamy and rich deep within, this is a great cheese plate offering for the conundrum it creates with its presentation tableside.

AMARENA CHERRIES
(to buy, see page 266)

APRICOT
MOSTARDA

BLACK TRUFFLE
HONEY

Cheese Condiments

Apricot Mostarda

MAKES ABOUT 4 CUPS · PHOTO OPPOSITE

4 cups (about 1 pound) dried apricots, thinly sliced

¾ cup Simple Syrup (page 239)

½ cup dry white wine

1½ teaspoons hot red pepper flakes

1 tablespoon mustard seeds

1 tablespoon mustard oil (see Sources, page 266)

Combine the apricots, simple syrup, and wine in a medium pot and bring to a boil. Reduce the heat and simmer for 15 minutes to soften the apricots.

Transfer to a bowl and stir in the pepper flakes, mustard seeds, and mustard oil. Let cool, then cover and refrigerate overnight before serving. *(The mostarda can be refrigerated for up to 1 month.)*

Black Truffle Honey

MAKES ABOUT 2 CUPS · PHOTO OPPOSITE

2 cups honey

One 6-ounce can black truffle trimmings, drained

Combine the honey and truffles, mixing well. Stir in one of the flavorings listed below if desired. *(The honey can be refrigerated for up to 6 months; bring to room temperature before serving.)*

Variations: For each cup of honey, add 2 tablespoons toasted fennel seeds, 2 tablespoons crushed pink or green peppercorns, 1 tablespoon Szechuan peppercorns, or 3 tablespoons toasted caraway seeds.

Note: To toast seeds, heat them in a dry heavy skillet over medium heat until fragrant and very slightly darker, about 3 minutes. Transfer to a plate to cool.

INSALATA

There is no question

that, as a category, the most nourishing and healthy things to eat from the entire world of soil and gardens are the edible leafy foliage and greens that live in the sun above the earth itself. High in content of just about everything good for you, including calcium, unstorable vitamin C, vitamin E, beta-carotene, and fiber, they are low in calories, have no cholesterol, and are fat free. They are crunchy and crisp if you want them to be, but they also perform well when wilted with a warm dressing or sitting under a small portion of protein—meat, fish, or grains. They are a virtual kitchen-pantry painter's palette in that they are totally adaptable to almost any dish and, better than that, no one has ever told you to eat less salad! The following are some of our favorites, and the ingredients in these recipes can be substituted in and out at will for anything that looks better or fresher or is in season wherever you are. There are very few vegetables that we do not like both raw and cooked, so feel free to experiment with both sides of the coin—almost anything goes.

106

**Radicchio &
Ginger Salad**

RECIPE PAGE 112

107

Asparagus & Pecorino Salad

RECIPE PAGE 113

108

**Romaine &
Red Onion Salad**

RECIPE PAGE 113

109

Three-Bean Salad

RECIPE PAGE 114

110

Summer Caprese Salad

RECIPE PAGE 115

111

Misticanza

RECIPE PAGE 115

Radicchio & Ginger Salad

SERVES 6 · PHOTO PAGE 106

2 ounces young ginger, peeled

1½ pounds radicchio, cored and each head cut into 8 wedges

¼ cup balsamic vinegar

1 teaspoon sugar

¼ cup lemon agrumato oil (see Sources, page 266) or ¼ cup extra virgin olive oil plus a generous pinch of grated lemon zest

¼ cup extra virgin olive oil

Maldon or other flaky sea salt and coarsely ground black pepper

Using a Benriner (Japanese mandoline) or other vegetable slicer, thinly slice the ginger; or slice it paper-thin with a very sharp knife. Combine the radicchio and ginger in a large bowl, tossing gently.

Whisk the vinegar and sugar together in a small bowl. Whisk in the oils, then whisk in salt and pepper to taste.

Toss the salad with half the vinaigrette, and serve the remainder on the side.

Asparagus & Pecorino Salad

SERVES 6 · PHOTO PAGE 107

1 pound asparagus, tough bottom ends snapped off

2 to 3 ounces pecorino romano

¼ cup Lemon Vinaigrette (page 24)

Kosher salt and coarsely ground black pepper

Using a Benriner (Japanese mandoline) or other vegetable slicer, or a vegetable peeler, thinly shave the asparagus, making long diagonal shavings. Transfer to a medium bowl.

Shave or thinly slice the pecorino and add to the bowl. Drizzle with half the vinaigrette, season lightly with salt and pepper, and toss gently. Serve with the remaining vinaigrette on the side.

Romaine & Red Onion Salad

SERVES 6 · PHOTO PAGE 108

2 heads romaine, tough outer green leaves removed, remaining leaves cut or torn into bite-sized pieces

1½ tablespoons red wine vinegar

3 tablespoons extra virgin olive oil

Maldon or other flaky sea salt and coarsely ground black pepper

2 ounces cacio di Roma, cut into 6 thin slices, plus a chunk (optional) for grating

1 small red onion, sliced into paper-thin rings

Soak the romaine in a bowl of cool water for 10 minutes to crisp it. Drain and spin dry. Transfer to a large bowl.

Whisk the vinegar and oil together in a small bowl. Drizzle the romaine with half the vinaigrette, tossing to coat, and season with salt and pepper.

Divide the romaine among six salad bowls and add a slice of cheese to each. Grate additional cheese over the romaine if desired and garnish with the red onion. Serve the remaining vinaigrette on the side.

Three-Bean Salad

SERVES 6 · PHOTO PAGE 109

Kosher salt

1 pound green beans

One 15-ounce can chickpeas, rinsed and drained

One 15-ounce can white kidney beans (cannellini), rinsed and drained

⅓ cup coarsely chopped fresh mint

½ cup Red Wine Vinaigrette (page 23)

Maldon or other flaky sea salt and coarsely ground black pepper

Bring 4 quarts of water to a boil in a large pot and add 2 tablespoons kosher salt. Add the beans and blanch until crisp-tender, about 3 minutes. Drain in a colander and cool under cold running water; drain well.

Combine the green beans, chickpeas, and kidney beans in a large bowl. Add the mint and toss well. Add half the vinaigrette and toss again. Season with Maldon salt and pepper. Serve, or let stand at room temperature for 1 hour to bring out the flavors.

Serve the salad with the remaining vinaigrette on the side.

Misticanza

SERVES 6 · PHOTO PAGE 111

1 small fennel bulb, trimmed

8 ounces radishes, trimmed

8 ounces (2 medium bunches) arugula, trimmed, washed, and spun dry

6 tablespoons Lemon Vinaigrette (page 24)

Maldon or other flaky sea salt and coarsely ground black pepper

Using a Benriner (Japanese mandoline) or other vegetable slicer, thinly shave the fennel. Transfer to a medium bowl.

Thinly shave the radishes and add to the bowl. Add the arugula and toss gently. Drizzle with half the vinaigrette, tossing gently. Season with salt and pepper, and serve with the remaining vinaigrette on the side.

Summer Caprese Salad

SERVES 6 · PHOTO PAGE 110

10 ounces fresh mozzarella

1½ pounds assorted ripe tomatoes (choose a combination of colors, types, and sizes), such as Brandywine, purple Cherokee, cherry, pear, peach, and/or Green Zebra

2 tablespoons champagne vinegar

6 tablespoons extra virgin olive oil

1 small bunch basil (Genovese, lemon, Thai, or fino verde), leaves removed, or about 1 cup mixed fresh basil leaves

Maldon or other flaky sea salt

With a sharp knife, cut the mozzarella into ½-inch-thick slices. Transfer to a serving platter, reserving any milky liquid from the cheese in a small cup.

If using cherry or grape tomatoes, cut them in half; reserve the juices. Core the remaining tomatoes and slice them, reserving the juices. Arrange the tomatoes on the cheese.

Whisk the vinegar, reserved tomato juices, any liquid from the mozzarella, and the olive oil together in a small bowl.

Tear the basil leaves over the salad. Pour the vinaigrette over it, sprinkle with salt, and serve.

116

Arugula with Tomato Raisins

RECIPE PAGE 125

117

Pumpkin & Mushroom Salad

RECIPE PAGE 124

118

Shaved Fall
Fruit Salad

RECIPE PAGE 126

119

Tricolore Salad

WITH PARMIGIANO-REGGIANO

RECIPE PAGE 126

120

Celery &
Pancetta Salad

RECIPE PAGE 127

121

Winter Caprese Salad

RECIPE PAGE 128

122

Zach's Escarole Salad

RECIPE PAGE 129

123

Beet Salad

WITH ROBIOLA

RECIPE PAGE 129

Pumpkin & Mushroom Salad

SERVES 6 · PHOTO PAGE 117

1 small butternut squash (about 1¼ pounds), peeled, cut lengthwise in half, seeded, and cut into ½-inch pieces

8 ounces baby shiitake mushroom caps, left whole, or larger mushroom caps, cut into ¼-inch-thick slices

3 large shallots, cut into ¼-inch dice

¼ cup extra virgin olive oil

Maldon or other flaky sea salt and coarsely ground black pepper

1 ounce canned sliced black truffles in oil or 1 tablespoon extra virgin olive oil

2 tablespoons balsamic vinegar

Juice of 1 lemon

1 teaspoon minced fresh rosemary

4 ounces cremini mushrooms, trimmed and thinly sliced

Preheat the broiler. Combine the squash, shiitake mushrooms, and shallots in a large bowl. Add the oil, tossing to coat. Season with salt and pepper. Spread the vegetables out on a large baking sheet and broil, stirring occasionally, until the squash is slightly charred and just tender, 15 to 20 minutes. Transfer to a serving bowl.

Meanwhile, mince the truffles, if using (reserve the oil). Whisk the balsamic vinegar, lemon juice, truffles, with their oil (or the 1 tablespoon oil), and rosemary together in a small bowl.

Scatter the cremini over the warm salad and add the vinaigrette, tossing to coat. Serve warm or at room temperature.

Arugula with Tomato Raisins

SERVES 6 · PHOTO PAGE 116

1 pound (3 large bunches) arugula, trimmed, washed, and spun dry

About ¼ cup Lemon Vinaigrette (page 24)

Maldon or other flaky sea salt and coarsely ground black pepper

Tomato Raisins (recipe follows)

Toss the arugula with just enough vinaigrette to coat in a large bowl. Season with salt and pepper.

Transfer the arugula to a serving bowl or platter, garnish with the tomatoes, and serve.

TOMATO RAISINS

MAKES ABOUT ⅔ CUP

1 pint (about 2 cups) cherry or grape tomatoes

1 tablespoon extra virgin olive oil

Maldon or other flaky sea salt

Preheat the oven to 250°F. Line a heavy baking sheet with parchment paper or foil.

Toss the tomatoes with the oil in a bowl. Sprinkle lightly with salt and toss again. Spread out on the baking sheet and bake for 3½ to 4 hours, stirring and turning the tomatoes occasionally, until they are lightly browned in spots and shriveled (as the tomatoes bake, they will puff up and then deflate—to test for doneness, remove a tomato from the oven and let cool briefly: if it shrinks and shrivels, the tomatoes are done).

Shaved Fall Fruit Salad

SERVES 6 · PHOTO PAGE 118

1 medium cucumber

2 medium summer squash

1 small melon, such as Cavaillon, quartered, seeded, and peeled

2 Gala or McIntosh apples

12 grapes, halved or quartered, seeded if necessary

¼ cup agresto or other verjuice (see Sources, page 266)

¼ cup extra virgin olive oil

Maldon or other flaky sea salt and coarsely ground black pepper

Using a Benriner (Japanese mandoline) or other vegetable slicer, thinly slice the cucumber, and transfer to a large serving bowl. Thinly slice the squash and add to the bowl. Thinly slice the melon and add to the bowl. Thinly slice the apples, avoiding the cores, and add to the bowl. Add the grapes, tossing gently to mix the fruit and vegetables.

Whisk the agresto and oil together in a small bowl. Season with salt and pepper. Add half the vinaigrette to the fruit and vegetables, tossing gently. Serve with the remaining vinaigrette on the side.

Tricolore Salad with Parmigiano-Reggiano

SERVES 6 · PHOTO PAGE 119

1 pound arugula (3 large bunches), trimmed, washed, and spun dry

2 heads Belgian endive, cored and cut into ¾-inch-wide slices

1 large head radicchio, cored and coarsely chopped

6 tablespoons Lemon Vinaigrette (page 24)

Maldon or other flaky sea salt and coarsely ground black pepper

A 4-ounce chunk of Parmigiano-Reggiano for shaving

Combine all the lettuces in a large bowl, tossing to mix. Drizzle with half the vinaigrette, tossing gently. Season with salt and pepper.

Transfer the salad to a serving bowl, shave the cheese over it, and serve with the remaining vinaigrette on the side.

Celery & Pancetta Salad

SERVES 6 · PHOTO PAGE 120

4 ounces pancetta, cut into ¼-inch dice (have the pancetta sliced ¼ inch thick when you buy it)

2 tablepoons extra virgin olive oil

1 pound celery root (celeriac), trimmed and peeled

4 tender inner celery ribs, sliced paper-thin

¼ cup slivered celery leaves (chiffonade)

6 tablespoons Red Wine Vinaigrette (page 23)

Maldon or other flaky sea salt and coarsely ground black pepper

Combine the pancetta and olive oil in a medium sauté pan and cook over medium heat, stirring occasionally, until the pancetta has rendered its fat and is crisp, 5 to 7 minutes.

Meanwhile, using a box grater, coarsely grate the celery root into a large bowl. Add the sliced celery and celery leaves.

Add the vinaigrette to the salad, tossing gently. Season with salt and pepper. Pour the pancetta, with the rendered fat, over the salad, tossing gently, and serve immediately.

Winter Caprese Salad

SERVES 6 · PHOTO PAGE 121

Oven-Dried Tomatoes (recipe follows), halved

¼ cup agrodolce (see page 254)

6 tablespoons Basil Pesto (page 172)

Six 3-ounce balls fresh mozzarella (or a generous 1 pound fresh mozzarella, cut into 6 slices)

Combine the tomatoes and agrodolce in a small bowl, mixing well.

Put the pesto in a small bowl. Dip each mozzarella ball into the pesto, coating it generously, and place on a salad plate. Divide the tomatoes among the plates and serve.

OVEN-DRIED TOMATOES

MAKES ABOUT 1½ CUPS

2½ pounds plum tomatoes

1 tablespoon extra virgin olive oil

½ teaspoon Maldon or other flaky sea salt

Preheat the oven to 350°F. Line a heavy baking sheet with parchment paper or foil.

Cut the tomatoes lengthwise in half and scoop out the seeds and pulp with your fingers. Toss the tomatoes with the olive oil and salt in a bowl, then arrange cut side down on the baking sheet.

Bake the tomatoes for 30 minutes, or until the skins are beginning to shrivel. Remove from the oven and let cool slightly. Reduce the oven temperature to 250°F.

Pull off the tomato skins and discard. Blot up any juices on the baking sheet. Roast the tomatoes for 1½ to 2 hours, or until the tomatoes are collapsed and slightly wrinkled but still moist. Let cool. *(The tomatoes can be refrigerated for up to 3 days.)*

Zach's Escarole Salad

SERVES 6 · PHOTO PAGE 122

2 heads escarole, tough outer green leaves removed, remaining leaves torn into bite-sized pieces

5 sunchokes, scrubbed and thinly sliced

½ cup blanched whole almonds, toasted (see page 261) and ground or finely chopped

½ cup coarsely grated Tuscan caciotta or cacio di Roma

6 tablespoons Lemon Vinaigrette (page 24)

Maldon or other flaky salt and coarsely ground black pepper

Soak the escarole in a bowl of cool water for 10 minutes to crisp it. Drain and spin dry.

Combine the sunchokes, almonds, and cheese in a large bowl, tossing to mix. Add the escarole, tossing gently. Drizzle with half the vinaigrette, tossing to coat. Season with salt and pepper.

Transfer the salad to a serving bowl and serve with the remaining vinaigrette on the side.

Beet Salad with Robiola

SERVES 6 · PHOTO PAGE 123

2 large bunches beets with greens

1 tablespoon olive oil

¾ cup beet juice (from a health food store)

¼ cup Red Wine Vinaigrette (page 23)

Maldon or other flaky sea salt

6 ounces creamy robiola (robiola di Piemonte)

Preheat the oven to 400°F.

Cut off the beet greens and reserve half of them. Cut enough of the stems into ¼-inch slices to make ¼ cup. Scrub the beets, toss with the olive oil, and spread in a baking pan. Roast until tender, 50 to 60 minutes. Let cool slightly, then rub off the skins.

Meanwhile, bring the beet juice to a boil in a saucepan and boil until reduced to 2 tablespoons. Cool, then whisk in the vinaigrette.

Cut the beets into 1-inch chunks and transfer to a large bowl. Leave small beet greens whole; cut larger leaves into ½-inch-wide strips. Add the beet greens and stems to the beets and toss with enough vinaigrette to coat lightly. Season with salt. Transfer to a serving platter, dollop with the robiola, and serve.

PASTA

The good news is that

we have survived the low-carb pestilence, the monochromatic diet that seemed to work because Americans had become so carbohydrate-dependent that any reduction in carbs was a direct reduction in what they ate. And, of course, less food or fewer calories on a daily basis will usually result in weight loss. But the real answer to healthy weight maintenance is a combination of exercise and smart eating, something the Italians and other Europeans have done for centuries. Eating bad carbs makes no sense, while eating good carbs is an excellent way to enjoy a delicious and filling meal with less protein and fat. The key is to understand how much pasta to make and eat and how much of the corresponding sauce or condiment to serve with it.

As I have written a thousand times and said a million, the Italians eat their pasta quite al dente and sauced in a very light and minimal way. If there is ever a lot of extra sauce in the pan when you are about to plate the pasta, grab the pasta out of the pan with tongs, or use a slotted spoon, and leave the extra sauce behind. I think you will see that the dish feels lighter, tastes more balanced, and generally leaves you feeling a little cleaner. The idea that the toasted wheat flavor of the pasta itself is the dish is foreign to many Americans, but when you taste and appreciate the mouth-feel of a perfectly cooked and dressed pasta dish, you will know and understand forever why Italy is such a great place both physically and emotionally, as the Italian culture of the table is so well conceived and executed. This is never more evident than in the world of the myriad pastas from region to region.

The recipes in this chapter, which are disarmingly easy to shop for and prepare, more represent the actual pasta dishes Italians eat at home every day, often twice a day. None of them require fresh handmade pasta; we make them with high-quality dried pasta from Italy, pasta that is still extruded through traditional bronze dies to give the noodles a rougher "cat's tongue" toothsome texture and quality. We love Barilla, De Cecco, Rustichella d'Abruzzo, and Setaro best, but there are literally hundreds of good pastas available at all levels of pricing and in all shapes and sizes.

TEN MOST IMPORTANT PASTA COOKING TIPS

Italians are pretty specific about how to cook and dress their noodles, and we urge you to adhere to our ten basic rules when cooking pasta.

• For each pound of pasta, use 6 quarts water and 3 tablespoons kosher salt. Don't salt the water before it has come to a boil, or it will take longer to boil.

• Use well-crafted extra virgin olive oil. Consider the region, nuance, clarity, and weight of the oil when choosing one for a pasta dish. (See page 261 for our favorites.)

• Never allow the oil to smoke. If necessary, remove the pan from the heat briefly.

• Never boil a sauce until you've added the pasta.

• The sauce should always be well integrated with the pasta, unctuous, as supple as silk, and homogenous.

• When finishing a pasta with a butter sauce, use cold butter for a better emulsion.

• For depth, freshness, and contrast, add fresh herbs or raw tomatoes after tossing the pasta with the sauce, and then finish with olive oil.

• Remove the pan of pasta and sauce from the heat before adding the cheese.

• Less is always more. It's more important for the sauce and pasta to be one, a sum greater than its parts. Fat and cheese are not as important as water and balance.

• Always plate pasta with the thought of its performance on the table in a few minutes.

The dishes that follow may be seen in simple regional osterie or trattorie. They are rarely served in fancy-pants ristoranti, because they are perceived as home-cooking fare (with the occasional splurge or two, in the case of caviar and truffles). That is exactly why we serve them at Otto—we like to eat like this, and our kids do too.

133

SPAGHETTI

with Butter or Garlic & Oil

RECIPES PAGES
140 & 141

134

SPAGHETTI WITH
Black & White Truffles

RECIPES PAGE 142

135

Spaghetti with Caviar

RECIPE PAGE 143

136

Spaghetti
with Glass Eels

RECIPE PAGE 143

137

Spaghetti alla Carbonara

RECIPE PAGE 144

138

SPAGHETTI
all'Amatriciana
& alla Gricia

RECIPES PAGES
145 & 146

139

Spaghetti
con la Sarde

RECIPE PAGE 147

Spaghetti with Garlic & Oil

SERVES 6 · PHOTO PAGE 133

Kosher salt

6 tablespoons extra virgin olive oil

10 garlic cloves, thinly sliced

1 teaspoon hot red pepper flakes

¼ cup finely chopped fresh Italian parsley

1 pound spaghetti

Freshly grated Parmigiano-Reggiano
   for serving

Bring 6 quarts of water to a boil in a large pot and add 3 tablespoons kosher salt.

Meanwhile, combine the olive oil and garlic in another large pot and cook over medium heat, stirring occasionally, until the garlic is just beginning to brown lightly, 2 to 3 minutes. Stir in the red pepper flakes and parsley and remove from the heat.

Drop the pasta into the boiling water and cook until just al dente. Drain, reserving about ½ cup of the pasta water.

Return the garlic oil to medium heat, add the pasta and ¼ cup of the reserved pasta water, and stir and toss over medium heat to coat the pasta well (add a splash or two more of the reserved pasta water if necessary to loosen the sauce). Serve immediately, with grated Parmigiano on the side.

Spaghetti with Butter

SERVES 6 · PHOTO PAGE 133

Kosher salt

1 pound spaghetti

6 tablespoons cold unsalted butter, cut into small chunks

Coarsely ground black pepper

Freshly grated Parmigiano-Reggiano for serving

Bring 6 quarts of water to a boil in a large pot and add 3 tablespoons kosher salt. Drop the pasta into the boiling water and cook just until al dente.

Drain the pasta, reserving ½ cup of the pasta water. Pour the reserved pasta water into another large pot and bring just to a boil. Reduce the heat and whisk in the butter bit by bit, without letting it melt completely, until you have a light, creamy sauce. Add the pasta and stir and toss to coat well. Remove from the heat and season with pepper. Serve immediately, with grated Parmigiano on the side.

OUR FAVORITE OLIVE OILS

ITALIAN RIVIERA
These are delicate and light, with a grassy fragrance and less viscosity than the Tuscan oils.
· Ceppo Antico
· Alex Nember
· Rosmarino
· Vittorio Cassini

TUSCANY
More intensely "green" in color and flavor, these are more powerful players in any dish.
· Tenuta di Capezzana
· La Mozza
· Frescobaldi Laudemio
· Castello di Ama
· Badia a Coltibuono
· Volpaia

SICILY
These are potentially similar to Tuscan oils, but they are available fresher in late winter because of their January harvest schedule.
· Trappitu
· Frantoi Cutrera Primo
· Olio Verde
· Geraci

HEALDSBURG, CALIFORNIA
This is very much like a Tuscan oil—in fact, the olive trees came from Tuscany.
· DaVero

Spaghetti with White Truffles

SERVES 6 · PHOTO PAGE 134

Kosher salt

1 pound spaghetti

10 tablespoons (1¼ sticks) cold unsalted butter, cut into small chunks

2 ounces fresh white truffles

Bring 6 quarts water to a boil in a large pot and add 3 tablespoons kosher salt. Drop in the pasta and cook until just al dente.

Drain the pasta, reserving ⅔ cup of the pasta water. Pour the reserved pasta water into another large pot, add the butter, and bring to a boil, whisking to emulsify the sauce. Add the pasta and stir and toss to coat well.

Transfer the pasta to a serving bowl, shave the truffles over it, and serve immediately.

Spaghetti with Black Truffles

SERVES 6 · PHOTO PAGE 134

Kosher salt

10 tablespoons (1¼ sticks) unsalted butter

2 ounces canned sliced black truffles in oil, drained

1 pound spaghetti

2 ounces cacio di Roma, grated

Bring 6 quarts water to a boil in a large pot and add 3 tablespoons kosher salt.

Meanwhile, melt the butter in another large pot over medium-high heat, and cook until the butter begins to brown and smell fragrant, about 2 minutes. Stir in the truffles and remove from the heat.

Drop the pasta into the boiling water and cook until just al dente. Drain, reserving about ½ cup of the pasta water.

Add the pasta and ¼ cup of the reserved pasta water to the truffle butter and stir and toss over medium heat until the pasta is well coated (add a splash or two more of the reserved pasta water if necessary to loosen the sauce). Transfer the pasta to a serving bowl and serve immediately.

Spaghetti with Caviar

SERVES 6 · PHOTO PAGE 135

Kosher salt

¼ cup extra virgin olive oil

4 tablespoons unsalted butter

1 pound spaghetti

Caviar—as much as you are willing to use
(we like osetra from Russ & Daughters;
see Sources, page 266)

Bring 6 quarts of water to a boil in a large
pot and add 3 tablespoons kosher salt.

Meanwhile, combine the oil and butter in
another large pot and heat over medium
heat until the butter is melted. Remove
from the heat.

Drop the pasta into the boiling water and
cook until just al dente. Drain, reserving
about ½ cup of the pasta water.

Add the pasta and ¼ cup of the reserved
pasta water to the butter mixture and stir
and toss over medium heat until the pasta
is well coated (add a splash or two more
of the reserved pasta water if necessary to
loosen the sauce). Transfer the pasta to a
serving bowl, garnish with the caviar, and
serve immediately.

Spaghetti with Glass Eels

SERVES 6 · PHOTO PAGE 136

Kosher salt

6 tablespoons extra virgin olive oil

5 garlic cloves, smashed and peeled

1 pound spaghetti

8 ounces fresh or frozen glass eels, thawed
if frozen (see Note)

Bring 6 quarts of water to a boil in a large
pot and add 3 tablespoons kosher salt.

Meanwhile, heat the olive oil in a large pot
over medium heat. Add the garlic and sauté
until lightly golden, 1 to 2 minutes. Remove
from the heat.

Drop the pasta into the boiling water and
cook until just al dente. Drain, reserving
¼ cup of the pasta water.

Add the glass eels to the garlic oil and heat
over medium-high heat, stirring, until they
are opaque. Add the pasta, tossing and
stirring to mix well (add a splash of the
reserved pasta water if necessary to loosen
the sauce). Serve immediately.

*Note: Glass eels are in season for a few weeks
in the spring, when you should be able to find
them in a local Chinatown.*

Spaghetti alla Carbonara

SERVES 6 · PHOTO PAGE 137

Kosher salt

5 ounces sliced pancetta, cut into ½-inch-
  wide strips

¼ cup extra virgin olive oil

1 tablespoon coarsely ground black pepper

6 fresh large eggs

1 pound spaghetti

½ cup freshly grated Parmigiano-Reggiano,
  plus extra for serving

¼ cup grated pecorino romano

Bring 6 quarts of water to a boil in a large
pot and add 3 tablespoons kosher salt.

Meanwhile, combine the pancetta and oil in
another large pot and cook over medium-
high heat until the pancetta has rendered
some of its fat and is lightly browned, about
7 minutes. Stir in the pepper and remove
from the heat.

Separate the eggs, being careful to keep
the yolks intact, putting the whites in a
small bowl and the yolks in a shallow dish.

Drop the pasta into the boiling water and
cook until just al dente. Drain, reserving
⅔ cup of the pasta water.

Add the reserved pasta water to the pancetta and bring to a simmer over medium
heat. Add the egg whites and cook, whisking
furiously, until they are frothy but not set,
about 1 minute. Add the pasta, stirring and
tossing well to coat. Stir in the cheeses.

Divide the pasta among six bowls, making
a nest in the center of each portion. Gently
drop an egg yolk into each nest and serve
immediately, advising your guests to stir
the yolk into the pasta so it will cook. Pass
additional grated Parmigiano on the side.

Spaghetti all'Amatriciana

SERVES 6 · PHOTO PAGE 138

Kosher salt

¼ cup extra virgin olive oil

4 ounces sliced guanciale or pancetta, or
good American bacon, cut into ½-inch-
wide strips

1 medium red onion, halved lengthwise,
ends trimmed, and cut lengthwise into
¼-inch-wide slices

¼ cup tomato paste

1½ to 2 teaspoons hot red pepper flakes

¾ cup Pomì strained tomatoes, simmered
until reduced by half

1 pound spaghetti

½ cup freshly grated Parmigiano-Reggiano,
plus extra for serving

½ cup grated pecorino romano

⅓ cup coarsely chopped fresh Italian parsley

Bring 6 quarts of water to a boil in a large
pot and add 3 tablespoons kosher salt.

Meanwhile, combine the oil, guanciale, and
onion in another large pot and cook over
medium-high heat, stirring frequently, until
the guanciale is lightly browned and the
onion is softened, about 7 minutes. Stir
in the tomato paste and red pepper flakes
and cook, stirring, until fragrant, about
1 minute. Stir in the tomato sauce and
remove from the heat.

Drop the pasta into the boiling water and
cook until just al dente. Drain, reserving
about ½ cup of the pasta water.

Add the pasta and ¼ cup of the reserved
pasta water to the guanciale and stir and
toss over medium heat until the pasta is
well coated (add a splash or two more of
the reserved pasta water if necessary to
loosen the sauce). Stir in the cheeses and
parsley and serve immediately, with additional grated Parmigiano on the side.

Spaghetti alla Gricia

SERVES 6 · PHOTO PAGE 138

Kosher salt

¼ cup extra virgin olive oil

4 ounces sliced guanciale or pancetta, or good American bacon, cut into ½-inch-wide strips

1 medium red onion, halved lengthwise, ends trimmed, and cut lengthwise into ¼-inch-wide slices

1 tablespoon coarsely ground black pepper

1 pound spaghetti

½ cup freshly grated Parmigiano-Reggiano, plus extra for serving

½ cup grated pecorino romano

⅓ cup coarsely chopped fresh Italian parsley

Bring 6 quarts of water to a boil in a large pot and add 3 tablespoons kosher salt.

Meanwhile, combine the oil, guanciale, and onion in another large pot and cook over medium-high heat, stirring frequently, until the guanciale is lightly browned and the onion is softened, about 7 minutes. Stir in the pepper and remove from the heat.

Drop the pasta into the boiling water and cook until just al dente. Drain, reserving about ½ cup of the pasta water.

Add the pasta and ¼ cup of the reserved pasta water to the guanciale and stir and toss over medium heat until the pasta is well coated (add a splash or two more of the reserved pasta water if necessary to loosen the sauce). Stir in the cheeses and parsley and serve immediately, with additional grated Parmigiano on the side.

Spaghetti con la Sarde

SERVES 6 · PHOTO PAGE 139

1¼ pounds fresh sardines or 6 ounces good canned sardines from Spain

1 large fennel bulb

Kosher salt

6 tablespoons extra virgin olive oil

1 tablespoon fennel seeds

1 pound spaghetti

1 teaspoon fennel pollen (optional)

2 teaspoons minced or grated orange zest

½ cup coarse fresh bread crumbs, fried in olive oil until golden brown (see page 257)

If using fresh sardines, scrape off any scales with a blunt knife; cut off the fins. Cut off the head and tail of each fish and slit it open down the stomach. Pull out the backbone and the guts (a messy job but quite easy). Open out the fish, and cut the two fillets apart. Rinse the sardines well under cold water to remove any blood, and pat dry. Coarsely chop the sardines (fresh or canned).

Trim the fennel bulb, and reserve the fronds. Halve and core the fennel bulb and cut into ¼-inch dice. Chop enough of the reserved fronds to make ¼ cup, and reserve for garnish.

Bring 6 quarts of water to a boil in a large pot and add 3 tablespoons kosher salt.

Meanwhile, heat ¼ cup of the oil in another large pot over medium heat. Add the fennel seeds and cook, stirring, until fragrant and lightly toasted, about 1 minute. Add the diced fennel and cook, stirring occasionally, until softened, about 5 minutes. Add the sardines and cook, stirring occasionally, until just opaque throughout, 1 to 2 minutes. Remove from the heat.

Drop the pasta into the boiling water and cook until just al dente. Drain, reserving about ½ cup of the pasta water.

Add the pasta and ¼ cup of the reserved pasta water to the sardines and stir and toss over medium heat until the pasta is well coated (add a splash or two more of the reserved pasta water if necessary to loosen the sauce). Stir in the remaining 2 tablespoons olive oil, then stir in half of the chopped fennel fronds, half the fennel pollen, if using, half the orange zest, and half the bread crumbs.

Transfer the pasta to a serving bowl and scatter the remaining fennel fronds, pollen, zest, and bread crumbs over the top. Serve immediately.

Linguine with Cacio e Pepe

SERVES 6 · PHOTO OPPOSITE

Kosher salt

¼ cup coarsely ground black pepper

6 tablespoons extra virgin olive oil

6 tablespoons unsalted butter

1 pound dried linguine

¼ cup freshly grated Parmigiano-Reggiano, plus extra for serving

¼ cup grated pecorino romano

Bring 6 quarts water to a boil in a large pot and add 3 tablespoons kosher salt.

Meanwhile, set another large pot over medium heat, add the pepper, and toast, stirring, until fragrant, about 20 seconds. Add the oil and butter and stir occasionally until the butter has melted. Remove from the heat.

Drop the pasta into the boiling water and cook until just al dente. Drain, reserving about ½ cup of the pasta water.

Add ¼ cup of the reserved pasta water to the oil and butter mixture, then add the pasta and stir and toss over medium heat until the pasta is well coated. Stir in the cheeses (add a splash or two more of the reserved pasta water if necessary to loosen the sauce) and serve immediately, with additional grated Parmigiano on the side.

149

Linguine with Cacio e Pepe

RECIPE OPPOSITE

150

**Linguine
with Lemon**

RECIPE PAGE 158

151

Linguine with Mussels & Saffron

RECIPE PAGE 159

152

Linguine with Squid & Its Ink

RECIPE PAGE 160

153

Linguine with Zucchini & Bottarga

RECIPE PAGE 161

154

Linguine with Clams

RECIPE PAGE 162

155

Penne with Pomodoro Cotto & Crudo

RECIPES PAGES
163 & 164

156

Penne all'Arrabbiata

RECIPE PAGE 164

157

Penne alla Puttanesca

RECIPE PAGE 165

Linguine with Lemon

SERVES 6 · PHOTO PAGE 150

4 lemons, preferably Meyer or Sorrento

Kosher salt

6 tablespoons extra virgin olive oil

4 tablespoons unsalted butter

1 pound dried linguine

½ cup freshly grated Parmigiano-Reggiano,
plus extra for serving

Grate the zest and squeeze the juice from 2 of the lemons. Using a sharp serrated or other knife, cut off the tops and bottoms of the remaining 2 lemons to expose the flesh. Stand each lemon upright on the cutting board and cut away the peel and white pith in strips, working from top to bottom and following the natural curve of the fruit. Hold the fruit over a bowl to catch the juices and cut down along the membranes on either side of each section to release it, letting the sections drop into the bowl.

Bring 6 quarts of water to a boil in a large pot and add 3 tablespoons kosher salt.

Meanwhile, combine the lemon zest, juice, olive oil, and butter in another large pot and heat over medium-low heat until the butter melts. Remove from the heat.

Drop the pasta into the boiling water and cook until just al dente. Drain the pasta, reserving about ½ cup of the pasta water.

Add the pasta and ¼ cup of the reserved pasta water to the lemon juice mixture and stir and toss over medium heat to coat the pasta well. Stir in the lemon sections and cheese (add a splash or two more of the reserved pasta water if necessary to loosen the sauce) and serve immediately, with additional grated Parmigiano on the side.

Linguine with Mussels & Saffron

SERVES 6 · PHOTO PAGE 151

Kosher salt

⅓ cup extra virgin olive oil

3 garlic cloves, thinly sliced

1 tablespoon hot red pepper flakes

⅓ cup dry white wine

2 pounds PEI or other small mussels, scrubbed and debearded

1⅓ cups Oven-Dried Tomatoes (page 128), halved

Pinch of saffron threads

1 pound dried linguine

Bring 6 quarts of water to a boil in a large pot and add 3 tablespoons kosher salt.

Meanwhile, combine the oil and garlic in another large pot and cook over medium-high heat, stirring, just until the garlic is softened, about 1 minute. Add the red pepper flakes, wine, and mussels, cover, and steam until the mussels open, about 4 minutes; transfer the mussels to a bowl as they open. Stir the tomatoes and saffron into the mussel broth and remove the pot from the heat.

Drop the pasta into the boiling water and cook until just al dente. Drain, reserving about ⅔ cup of the pasta water.

Add the pasta and ⅓ cup of the reserved pasta water to the mussel broth and stir and toss over medium heat until the pasta is well coated (add a splash or two more of the reserved pasta water if necessary to loosen the sauce). Add the mussels and toss gently until warmed through. Serve immediately.

Linguine with Squid & Its Ink

SERVES 6 · PHOTO PAGE 152

Kosher salt

6 tablespoons extra virgin olive oil

5 garlic cloves, thinly sliced

½ cup dry white wine

¼ pound cleaned calamari

2 tablespoons squid ink (see Sources, page 266)

1 pound dried linguine

⅓ cup coarsely chopped fresh Italian parsley

½ lemon

Bring 6 quarts of water to a boil in a large pot and add 3 tablespoons kosher salt.

Meanwhile, combine the oil and garlic in another large pot and cook over medium heat, stirring, until the garlic is softened, about 1 minute. Add the wine, bring to a boil, and boil until reduced by half. Add the calamari and cook, stirring, until just tender, 2 to 3 minutes. Whisk in the squid ink and remove from the heat.

Drop the pasta into the boiling water and cook until just al dente. Drain, reserving about ½ cup of the pasta water.

Add the pasta and ¼ cup of the reserved pasta water to the sauce, stirring and tossing over medium heat, then cover and steam together over low heat for 2 minutes. Add a splash or two more of the reserved pasta water if necessary to loosen the sauce, stir in the parsley, and add a squeeze of lemon juice, or to taste. Serve immediately.

Linguine with Zucchini & Bottarga

SERVES 6 · PHOTO PAGE 153

Kosher salt

¼ cup extra virgin olive oil

1 medium red onion, halved lengthwise and thinly sliced

3 garlic cloves, sliced

8 ounces zucchini, halved lengthwise and cut into ⅓-inch-thick slices

8 ounces yellow squash, halved lengthwise and cut into ⅓-inch-thick slices

Maldon or other flaky sea salt

1½ to 2 teaspoons hot red pepper flakes

3 large fresh mint sprigs, leaves removed and torn into 2 or 3 pieces each

1½ cups Pomì strained tomatoes, simmered until reduced by half

1 pound dried linguine

½ cup coarse fresh bread crumbs, fried in olive oil until golden brown (see page 257)

A small piece of bottarga di mugine (see Sources, page 266)

Bring 6 quarts of water to a boil in a large pot and add 3 tablespoons kosher salt.

Meanwhile, heat the olive oil in another large pot over medium heat until hot. Add the red onion and cook, stirring, occasionally, until softened and golden brown, 8 to 10 minutes. Add the zucchini and yellow squash, season with Maldon salt, and cook, stirring occasionally, until softened, 8 to 10 minutes. Add the red pepper flakes, half the mint, and the tomato sauce and remove from the heat.

Drop the pasta into the boiling water and cook until just al dente. Drain, reserving about ¾ cup of the pasta water.

Add the pasta and ½ cup of the reserved pasta water to the sauce and stir and toss gently over medium heat until the pasta is well coated (add a splash or two more of the reserved pasta water if necessary to loosen the sauce). Transfer the pasta to a serving bowl and scatter the bread crumbs and the remaining mint over the top. Using a Microplane or other rasp grater, grate lots of bottarga over the top. Serve immediately.

Linguine with Clams

SERVES 6 · PHOTO PAGE 154

Kosher salt

6 tablespoons extra virgin olive oil

3 garlic cloves, minced

6 tablespoons dry white wine

1 tablespoon hot red pepper flakes

1 pound small clams, such as Manila, or cockles, scrubbed

1 pound dried linguine

⅓ cup coarsely chopped fresh Italian parsley

Bring 6 quarts water to a boil in a large pot and add 3 tablespoons kosher salt.

Meanwhile, combine the oil and garlic in a large pot and cook, stirring, over medium-high heat untl the garlic is softened, about 1 minute. Add the wine, red pepper flakes, and clams, cover, and cook, shaking the pot occasionally, until the clams open, about 5 minutes; transfer the clams to a bowl as they open. Remove the pot from the heat.

Drop the pasta into the boiling water and cook until just al dente. Drain, reserving about ½ cup of the pasta water.

Add the pasta and ¼ cup of the reserved pasta water to the clam broth and stir and toss over medium heat until the pasta is well coated (add a splash or two more of the reserved pasta water if necessary to loosen the sauce). Stir in the clams, with their juices, and toss until just heated through. Stir in the parsley and serve immediately.

Penne with Pomodoro Cotto

SERVES 6 · PHOTO PAGE 155

Kosher salt

6 tablespoons extra virgin olive oil

4 large garlic cloves, thinly sliced

2 cups Pomì chopped tomatoes

Maldon or other flaky sea salt and freshly ground black pepper

1 pound penne

Freshly grated Parmigiano-Reggiano for serving

Bring 6 quarts of water to a boil in a large pot and add 3 tablespoons kosher salt.

Meanwhile, heat 3 tablespoons of the olive oil in another large pot over medium heat until hot. Add the garlic and cook just until lightly golden, 1 to 2 minutes. Add the tomatoes, reduce the heat to medium-low, and cook, stirring for 5 minutes. Season with Maldon salt and pepper to taste and remove from the heat.

Drop the pasta into the boiling water and cook until just al dente. Drain, reserving about ½ cup of the pasta water.

Add the pasta and ¼ cup of the reserved pasta water to the tomatoes and stir and toss over medium heat until the pasta is well coated (add a splash or two more of the reserved pasta water if necessary to loosen the sauce). Stir in the remaining 3 tablespoons oil and serve immediately, with grated Parmigiano on the side.

Penne with Pomodoro Crudo

SERVES 6 · PHOTO PAGE 155

Kosher salt

1 pound penne

1 pound ripe tomatoes, cut into ½-inch dice

Pinch of sugar

Maldon or other flaky sea salt

6 tablespoons extra virgin olive oil

Freshly grated Parmigiano-Reggiano for serving

Bring 6 quarts water to a boil in a large pot and add 3 tablespoons kosher salt. Drop in the pasta and cook until just al dente. Drain the pasta, reserving about ½ cup of the pasta water.

Combine the tomatoes and ¼ cup of the reserved pasta water in another large pot and bring to a simmer over medium-high heat. Season the tomatoes with the sugar and Maldon salt to taste, add the pasta, and stir and toss over medium heat until the pasta is well coated (add a splash or two more of the reserved pasta water if necessary to loosen the sauce). Stir in the oil and serve immediately, with grated Parmigiano on the side.

Penne all'Arrabbiata

SERVES 6 · PHOTO PAGE 156

Kosher salt

¼ cup tomato paste

1 tablespoon hot red pepper flakes

1½ cups Pomì strained tomatoes, simmered until reduced by half

1 pound penne

¼ cup extra virgin olive oil

Maldon or other flaky sea salt

Freshly grated Parmigiano-Reggiano for serving

Bring 6 quarts of water to a boil in a large pot and add 3 tablespoons kosher salt.

Meanwhile, combine the tomato paste and pepper flakes in a large pot and stir over low heat just until fragrant. Stir in the tomato sauce and remove from the heat.

Drop the pasta into the boiling water and cook until just al dente. Drain the pasta, reserving ¾ cup of the pasta water.

Add the pasta and the reserved pasta water to the tomato sauce and stir and toss over medium heat until until the pasta is well coated. Season with salt if necessary, then add the oil, tossing well. Serve immediately, with grated Parmigiano on the side.

Penne alla Puttanesca

SERVES 6 · PHOTO PAGE 157

8 to 10 salt-packed anchovy fillets

Kosher salt

6 tablespoons extra virgin olive oil

½ medium red onion, cut into ¼-inch dice

4 garlic cloves, thinly sliced

1½ cups Pomì strained tomatoes, simmered until reduced by half

1½ to 2 teaspoons hot red pepper flakes

1 pound penne

2 tablespoons salt-packed capers, rinsed and soaked overnight in cold water (change the water frequently)

⅓ cup pitted Gaeta olives, coarsely chopped

⅓ cup coarsely chopped fresh Italian parsley

Freshly grated Parmigiano-Reggiano for serving

Put the anchovies in a small bowl and set it in the sink under a stream of cold running water for 20 minutes. Drain the anchovies, pat dry, and coarsely chop them.

Bring 6 quarts of water to a boil in a large pot and add 3 tablespoons kosher salt.

Meanwhile, combine the oil, onion, garlic, and anchovies in another large pot and cook over medium heat, stirring, until the onion is lightly browned and the anchovies have broken down, about 5 minutes. Add the tomato sauce and red pepper flakes and cook, stirring, until fragrant, about 3 minutes. Remove from the heat.

Drop the pasta into the boiling water and cook until just al dente. Drain, reserving ¾ cup of the pasta water.

Add the pasta and the reserved pasta water to the tomato mixture and stir and toss over medium heat until the pasta is well coated. Stirr in the capers, olives, and parsley and serve immediately, with grated Parmigiano on the side.

166

3 Pestos: Basil, Broccoli Rabe & Walnut

**RECIPES PAGES
172 & 173**

167

**Pennette with
Cauliflower Ragu**

RECIPE PAGE 174

168

Pennette with Summer Squash & Ricotta

RECIPE PAGE 176

169

Pennette with
Swiss Chard Ragu

RECIPE PAGE 177

170

Penne
alla Primavera

RECIPE PAGE 178

171

Penne alla Papalina

RECIPE PAGE 179

Pennette with 3 Pestos

SERVES 6 · PHOTO PAGE 166

Kosher salt

1 pound pennette

⅔ cup Basil, Walnut, or Broccoli Rabe Pesto (recipes follow)

Freshly grated Parmigiano-Reggiano for serving

Chopped walnuts for garnish if using Walnut Pesto

Bring 6 quarts of water to a boil in a large pot and add 3 tablespoons kosher salt. Drop in the pasta and cook until just al dente.

Drain the pasta, reserving ½ cup of the pasta water, and transfer to a serving bowl. Add the pesto and ¼ cup of the reserved pasta water and stir and toss until the pasta is well coated (add a splash or two more of the reserved pasta water if necessary to loosen the sauce). Serve immediately, with a sprinkling of walnuts if using walnut pesto, and grated Parmigiano on the side.

BASIL PESTO

MAKES ABOUT 1 CUP

3 garlic cloves

2 cups lightly packed fresh basil leaves

3 tablespoons pine nuts

Generous pinch of Maldon or other flaky sea salt

½ cup plus 2 tablespoons extra virgin olive oil

¼ cup freshly grated Parmigiano-Reggiano

3 tablespoons grated pecorino romano

With the motor running, drop the the garlic into a food processor to chop it. Add the basil, pine nuts, and salt and pulse until the basil and nuts are coarsely chopped, then process until finely chopped. With the motor running, drizzle in the oil. Transfer to a small bowl and stir in the Parmigiano and pecorino. *(The pesto can be stored in a tightly sealed jar, topped with a thin layer of extra virgin olive oil, for several weeks in the refrigerator.)*

WALNUT PESTO

MAKES ABOUT ¾ CUP

3 garlic cloves

1 cup walnuts, toasted (see page 261)

¼ cup extra virgin olive oil

¼ cup freshly grated Parmigiano-Reggiano

With the motor running, drop the the garlic into a food processor to chop it. Add the walnuts and pulse until coarsely chopped, then process until finely chopped; do not pulse to a paste. With the motor running, drizzle in the oil. Transfer to a small bowl and stir in the Parmigiano. *(The pesto can be stored in a tightly sealed jar, topped with a thin layer of extra virgin olive oil, for up to 1 week in the refrigerator.)*

BROCCOLI RABE PESTO

MAKES ABOUT 1 CUP

Kosher salt

½ pound broccoli rabe, stems trimmed

3 garlic cloves

¼ cup pine nuts, toasted (see page 261)

1 teaspoon Dijon mustard

6 tablespoons extra virgin olive oil

¼ cup freshly grated Parmigiano-Reggiano

Bring a large pot of water to a boil and add 2 tablespoons kosher salt. Add the broccoli rabe and cook until tender, about 7 minutes. Drain and transfer to a bowl of ice water to stop the cooking; drain well.

With the motor running, drop the garlic into a food processor and finely chop it. Add the broccoli rabe and pine nuts and pulse until finely chopped. Add the mustard and blend well. With the motor running, drizzle in the oil. Transfer to a small bowl and stir in the Parmigiano. *(The pesto can be stored in a tightly sealed jar, topped with a thin layer of extra virgin olive oil, for up to 1 week in the refrigerator.)*

Pennette with Cauliflower Ragu

SERVES 6 · PHOTO PAGE 167

1 medium cauliflower (about 2 pounds)

¼ cup extra virgin olive oil

1 medium white onion, cut into ¼-inch dice

3 garlic cloves, smashed and peeled

Maldon or other flaky sea salt

1½ to 2 teaspoons hot red pepper flakes

6 tablespoons unsalted butter, cut into
    6 pieces

Kosher salt

1 pound pennette

¾ cup freshly grated Parmigiano-Reggiano,
    plus extra for serving

½ cup coarse fresh bread crumbs, fried
    in olive oil until golden brown (see
    page 257)

1½ teaspoons minced fresh rosemary

Halve the cauliflower. Cut off the leaves and reserve them. Cut out the core and reserve it. Cut the cauliflower into small bite-sized florets, reserving the stalks. Chop the core, stalks, and leaves.

Combine the oil, onion, garlic, and cauliflower leaves, stalks, and core in a large pot, season with Maldon salt, and cook over medium heat, stirring frequently, until the leaves are just beginning to wilt, about 3 minutes. Reduce the heat to low and cook, stirring frequently, until the cauliflower leaves are just tender, 18 to 20 minutes.

Add the cauliflower florets, red pepper flakes, and 1 cup water and bring to a simmer over medium-high heat, then reduce the heat to a gentle simmer, cover, and cook, stirring occasionally, until the cauliflower is very soft and almost falling apart, 22 to 25 minutes. Add the butter, stirring gently until it melts, then season well with Maldon salt and remove from the heat. *(The cauliflower ragu can be prepared up to 3 days ahead. Let cool, then cover and refrigerate; reheat in a large pot over medium-low heat before adding the pasta.)*

Bring 6 quarts water to a boil in a large pot and add 3 tablespoons kosher salt. Drop in the pasta and cook until just al dente.

Drain the pasta, reserving about ⅔ cup of the pasta water. Add the pasta and ⅓ cup of the reserved pasta water to the cauliflower ragu and stir and toss over medium heat until the pasta is well coated (add a splash or two more of the reserved pasta water if necessary to loosen the sauce). Stir in the cheese.

Transfer the pasta to a serving bowl, sprinkle with the bread crumbs and rosemary, and serve, with additional grated cheese on the side.

Pennette with Summer Squash & Ricotta

SERVES 6 · PHOTO PAGE 168

Kosher salt

1 cup fresh ricotta

6 tablespoons extra virgin olive oil

½ cup freshly grated Parmigiano-Reggiano,
plus extra for serving

2 to 3 tablespoons warm water

1 pound summer squash or zucchini, or a
combination, cut lengthwise in half and
sliced into ⅓-inch-thick half-moons

Maldon or other flaky sea salt

1 pound pennette rigate

6 tablespoons coarsely chopped fresh mint

Coarsely ground black pepper

Bring 6 quarts of water to a boil in a large
pot and add 3 tablespoons kosher salt.

Meanwhile, whisk the ricotta and 3 tablespoons of the olive oil together in a small
bowl. Add the Parmigiano, whisking until
it is evenly incorporated. Whisk in 2 tablespoons warm water, then whisk in another
tablespoon of water if necessary to loosen
the consistency.

Heat the remaining 3 tablespoons olive oil
in a large pot over medium heat. Add the
squash and cook, stirring, until just tender
and golden brown, 4 to 5 minutes. Season
well with Maldon salt and remove from the
heat.

Drop the pasta into the boiling water and
cook until just al dente. Drain the pasta,
reserving ⅓ cup of the pasta water.

Add the pasta and the reserved pasta water
to the squash, stirring and tossing over
medium heat to mix well. Cover, reduce the
heat to low, and allow to steam together for
2 minutes.

Stir in the mint, season with Maldon salt if
necessary and with pepper, and transfer the
pasta to a serving bowl. Garnish with dollops of the whipped ricotta and serve immediately, with additional grated Parmigiano
on the side.

Pennette with Swiss Chard Ragu

SERVES 6 · PHOTO PAGE 169

¼ cup extra virgin olive oil

1 small white onion, halved and sliced
¼ inch thick

3 garlic cloves, smashed and peeled

1 pound Swiss chard, trimmed and sliced
¼ inch thick

Maldon or other flaky sea salt

4 tablespoons unsalted butter, cut into
4 pieces

Coarsely ground black pepper

Kosher salt

1 pound pennette

¾ cup freshly grated Parmigiano-Reggiano,
plus extra for serving

½ cup coarse fresh bread crumbs, fried
in olive oil until golden brown (see
page 257)

Combine the oil, onion, garlic, and chard in a large pot and cook over medium-high heat, stirring occasionally, until the onion and chard are beginning to soften, about 5 minutes. Season well with Maldon salt, add ¼ cup water, cover, reduce the heat to low, and cook, stirring occasionally, until the chard is very tender, about 20 minutes. Add the butter, stirring until it melts, then season with pepper and remove from the heat. *(The ragu can be prepared up to 2 days ahead. Let cool, then cover and refrigerate; reheat in a large pot over medium-low heat before adding the pasta.)*

Bring 6 quarts of water to a boil in a large pot and add 3 tablespoons kosher salt. Drop in the pasta and cook until just al dente.

Drain the pasta, reserving about ½ cup of the pasta water. Add the pasta and ¼ cup of the reserved pasta water to the chard ragu and stir and toss over medium heat until the pasta is well coated (add a splash or two more of the reserved pasta water if necessary to loosen the sauce). Stir in the cheese.

Transfer the pasta to a serving bowl and scatter the bread crumbs over the top. Serve with additional grated Parmigiano on the side.

Penne alla Primavera

SERVES 6 · PHOTO PAGE 170

6 tablespoons extra virgin olive oil

3 garlic cloves, thinly sliced

2 medium carrots, peeled, halved lengthwise, and sliced ¼ inch thick

4 ounces morels, halved if large, or cremini mushrooms, thinly sliced

8 ounces asparagus, stalks sliced ¼ inch thick on the bias, tips reserved separately

1 cup fresh or frozen peas, thawed if frozen

1 cup fava beans

4 scallions, white part only, thinly sliced

Maldon or other flaky sea salt and coarsely ground black pepper

Kosher salt

1 pound penne rigate

⅓ cup coarsely chopped fresh Italian parsley

⅓ cup coarsely chopped fresh basil

⅓ cup coarsely chopped fresh mint

Freshly grated Parmigiano Reggiano for serving

Heat ¼ cup of the oil in a large pot over medium-high heat until hot. Add the garlic and cook, stirring, until barely golden, 1 to 2 minutes. Add the carrots, reduce the heat to medium, and cook, stirring occasionally, until beginning to soften, about 4 minutes. Add the mushrooms and cook, stirring occasionally, until beginning to soften, about 3 minutes. Add the sliced asparagus and cook for 2 minutes, then add the asparagus tips, peas, fava beans, and scallions, season well with Maldon salt and pepper, and cook, stirring, until all the vegetables are just tender, about 2 minutes longer. Remove from the heat.

Bring 6 quarts of water to a boil in another large pot and add 3 tablespoons kosher salt. Drop the pasta into the boiling water and cook until just al dente. Drain the pasta, reserving ½ cup of the water.

Add the pasta and ¼ cup of the reserved pasta water to the vegetables, stirring and tossing over medium heat to mix well. Cover, reduce the heat to low, and allow to steam together for 2 minutes. Stir in the remaining 2 tablespoons olive oil and a splash or two more of the reserved pasta water if necessary to loosen the sauce, then stir in the herbs and serve immediately, with grated Parmigiano on the side.

Penne alla Papalina

SERVES 6 · PHOTO PAGE 171

Kosher salt

6 tablespoons extra virgin olive oil

8 ounces sliced prosciutto, cut into 1-inch squares

One 10-ounce package (2 cups) frozen peas, thawed

1 pound penne rigate

4 large eggs

1 cup freshly grated Parmigiano-Reggiano, plus extra for serving

Coarsely ground black pepper

Bring 6 quarts of water to a boil in a large pot and add 3 tablespoons kosher salt.

Meanwhile, combine 3 tablespoons of the oil and the prosciutto in another large pot and cook over medium-high heat, stirring occasionally, until the prosciutto has rendered some of its fat and is golden brown, about 5 minutes. Remove from the heat and stir in the peas.

Drop the pasta into the boiling water and cook until just al dente. Drain, reserving about ½ cup of the pasta water.

Whisk the eggs together in a medium bowl to break them up, then whisk in the remaining 3 tablespoons oil and ¼ cup of the reserved pasta water.

Add the pasta to the prosciutto and peas and stir and toss over medium heat to mix well. Add the egg mixture, remove from the heat, and stir and toss vigorously to slightly cook the eggs (add a splash or two more of the reserved pasta water if necessary to loosen the sauce). Stir in the Parmigiano, season with pepper, and serve immediately, with additional grated cheese on the side.

PIZZA

If there is one word

that describes what the world loves most about Italian food, it has to be a tie between *pasta* and . . . *pizza.* And while pasta in its infinite possibilities is relatively simple to prepare nearly perfectly at home, the cult of pizza makers, pizza fans, pizza freaks, pizza bloggers and writers, and just plain pizza lovers has together created a walled city within which lies the secret, nearly unachievable, almost never tasted or touched: perfect pizza. There are obsessives about the crust, and its simple but hugely important flour selection; about the tomato sauce; about the cheese and toppings; about the heat source and the cooking temperature; about the equipment, the floor surface, the pizza stone; about the coal-burning or wood-burning stove, the brick wall, and the gas options; and even about the brand of yeast.

There are regional variations in Italy from Naples to Rome, from Tuscany to Sardegna to Sicily. There are variations made in the U.S., from New York slices to Chicago deep-dish, from thin and crispy to the thick-crusted square pizza called Sicilian. There is even pizza made by a large chain with a cheese-stuffed crust and the possibility of adding pasta and French fries to the pizza as a topping. Suffice to say that in the following pages you will learn how to make what I consider to be the best pizza in the world, pizza with a soul, with a history, with a depth of flavor—and definitely without French fries. This is about our own take at Otto Pizzeria in NYC, a hybrid of New York thin-crust pizza with a crisp finish, not too puffy, light and pliant, that can be easily made in an American home kitchen with just a few pieces of equipment.

The recipes we call "classica" are based on traditional pies found at our favorite pizzerie in Italy. The "Otto" recipes are pizzas that we created for Otto within the framework of Italian food as we interpret it in NYC. We love our food simple and like to use flavorful things such as fennel or lardo, allowing them to sing their songs in unadorned ways. Like all great Italian food, pizza is a canvas upon which you should happily invent to your heart's desire (just leave out the kiwis, please). And when inventing your new creations, always be careful not to add too much stuff—simpler is better, and less is more.

And then there are our "kids'" pizzas. When we opened Otto, we immediately realized that our own families would be among our best customers, and in an effort to engage them, we asked each child to design his or her favorite pizza. To this day, the pizzas still stand, and one of them is served every day of the week, with each kid's name on the specials list. Some are more popular than others, but each has its own following.

Pizza Dough

MAKES ABOUT 2 POUNDS

Our dough is a little wetter than a standard bread dough, but this style produces the best results with our method of cooking: we use a hot griddle to parcook the pizza crusts. Our pan of choice is my own enameled cast-iron pizza griddle (see Sources, page 266), but you can also use a 10-inch enameled cast-iron frying or grilling pan or a smooth cast-iron pancake griddle.

1¼ cups warm water (95°F)

One ¼-ounce package active dry yeast

1½ teaspoons sugar

3½ cups "00" flour

Scant 2 tablespoons salt

¼ cup extra virgin olive oil

Semolina for dusting

TO MAKE THE DOUGH: Whisk the warm water, yeast, and sugar together in a bowl (PHOTO 1). Let stand in a warm place for 10 minutes, or until the yeast is foamy.

Combine the flour and salt in the bowl of a stand mixer fitted with the dough hook and mix well. With the mixer on low, add the yeast mixture and oil, mixing well (PHOTO 2). Continue to mix, gradually increasing the mixer speed to medium-high, until the dough is smooth and elastic. Transfer the dough to a lightly floured surface and give it a few turns by hand to finish kneading it; it will still be slightly sticky.

Alternatively, combine the flour and salt in a large bowl and whisk together. Make a well in the center of the dry ingredients and add the yeast mixture and oil. Using a wooden spoon, stir the wet ingredients into the dry ingredients until the mixture is too stiff to stir, then mix with your hands in the bowl until the dough comes together and pulls away from the sides of the bowl. Turn the dough out onto a lightly floured work surface and knead, adding only as much flour as necessary to prevent sticking, until smooth, elastic, and only slightly sticky. Transfer the dough to a large oiled bowl, turning to coat, cover with a kitchen towel or plastic wrap, and let rise in a warm place for 1 to 1½ hours, until doubled in size.

TO SHAPE THE DOUGH: Punch down the dough and turn it out onto a well-floured work surface. Divide it into 8 pieces (about 4 ounces each) and shape each one into a ball. Cover with a tea towel and let stand for 15 minutes before stretching the dough. Or, for easier handling, transfer the balls to a floured baking sheet and refrigerate until cold.

TO STRETCH AND PARBAKE THE DOUGH: Dust a large work surface with a mixture of flour and semolina. If the dough has been refrigerated, transfer one ball to the work surface and let stand just until still cool but not cold (about 60°F if tested with an instant-read thermometer).

Meanwhile, **PREHEAT THE GRIDDLE PAN** over medium heat until very hot, about 5 minutes (at the restaurant, we use a digital infrared thermometer to gauge the temperature of the griddle, which, ideally, should be 375°F).

Using your hands, begin to press and stretch the dough into a 9- to 10-inch round, adding only enough additional flour and semolina to the work surface to keep the dough from sticking (PHOTOS 3 & 4); using one hand as a guide, slope a slightly thicker rim all around the circle of dough. Work quickly, and be careful not to overwork the dough; if it resists or shrinks back as you shape it, let it rest briefly before proceeding. (If you prefer, you can roll out the dough with a rolling pin. Lightly flour the work surface and the rolling pin; sprinkle the rolling pin with more flour as necessary to prevent sticking.)

Carefully place the dough round on the preheated griddle pan (PHOTO 5) and cook until barely tan on the first side and browned in a few spots, 2 to 3 minutes. As the crust cooks, if you see any parts that remain undercooked, especially any thicker parts, simply press them against the pan so they cook a bit more; once the dough has set, you can move the crust around as necessary for more even cooking. Flip the crust over and cook until the second side is completely dry, about 1 minute longer.

Transfer the crust to a wire rack or a baking sheet, brushing off any excess flour, and allow to cool. Repeat with the remaining dough. (The parbaked crusts can be refrigerated overnight or frozen, well wrapped, for up to 2 weeks. Sometimes when you go through the effort of preparing all these steps, it might be worth making more than you may want to eat and then, depending on the toppings, freezing the extra finished pizzas. Occasionally I'll come home on a Sunday night and reheat a frozen pizza I made on Friday in the toaster oven—a great snack in less than 10 minutes, with absolutely no effort.)

We recommend making only one pizza at a time and serving each one as soon as it is done. If you need to make a lot for a large party, cook several of them once (slightly undercook them) and then reheat them in a warm oven before serving.

TO TOP EACH PIZZA AND BROIL IT: Place the parbaked pizza crust on a pizza peel or baking sheet (PHOTO 6). Spread the tomato sauce evenly over the crust, leaving a ½-inch border all around, and top with any remaining ingredients as specified in the individual recipe (PHOTO 7). (Do not put the sauce and any other ingredients on the pizza crust until ready to broil it, or the crust may become soggy.)

Slide the pizza under the broiler, about 4 inches from the heat source, and broil for 7 or 8 minutes (or as otherwise noted in the individual recipe), until the topping ingredients are heated and/or cooked through and the crust is charred and blistered in spots (PHOTO 8). Watch closely so that the ingredients don't burn, and move the pizza around or lower the broiler rack if necessary. (Sometimes during this stage, depending on the topping, the bottom may start to become soggy; if that happens, you can simply slip the pizza back onto the griddle momentarily to recrisp the crust.) And, if you prefer more color—as we do!—move the pizza closer to the heat source at the very end.

Finish the pizza with any remaining ingredients, as described in the individual recipe (PHOTO 9), and cut into slices with a pizza wheel, kitchen shears, or a very sharp knife. Serve hot.

Each topping recipe makes enough for one 9- to 10-inch pizza, and all of the recipes can be easily multiplied as desired.

IMPORTANT HINTS FOR PIZZA MAKING

Have all your equipment ready and accessible: measuring cups, a stand mixer or a large bowl and a wooden spoon, a whisk, a large bowl for rising the dough, your pizza griddle of choice. If you don't have a pizza peel, we recommend buying one—it will make the process easier and more fun. Set out a large cutting board for slicing the pizzas, and have a pizza wheel, kitchen shears, or a large sharp knife at hand. And, of course, plates to put the pizza on.

Create some extra clean work space in your kitchen; this will help keep you organized.

Measure all your ingredients before beginning the recipe.

Use a whisk to mix the yeast, sugar, and warm water to ensure that the ingredients are well mixed.

When combining the dry ingredients, give them a couple of whirls with the paddle attachment, or the whisk, to make sure they are evenly mixed.

This pizza dough becomes limp and very sticky the longer it is stretched, so work quickly when you are forming the crusts.

187

Marinara, Margherita D.O.P. & Romana

RECIPES PAGES 194 & 195

188
Napoletana
RECIPE PAGE 195

189

Quattro Formaggi

RECIPE PAGE 195

190

Sausage
& Peppers

RECIPE PAGE 196

191

Pepperoni

RECIPE PAGE 196

192

Quattro Stagioni

RECIPE PAGE 197

193

Prosciutto & Arugula

RECIPE PAGE 197

Classica

Romana

PHOTO PAGE 187

¼ cup Pomì strained tomatoes

1 tablespoon extra virgin olive oil

3 anchovy fillets, cut into 3 pieces each

1 tablespoon salt-packed capers, rinsed and soaked overnight in cold water (change the water often)

1 tablespoon thinly sliced red finger chile or serrano chile

½ cup shredded fresh mozzarella

Spread the tomato sauce evenly over the parbaked pizza crust, leaving a ½-inch border. Drizzle the oil over the sauce, arrange the anchovies on top, and sprinkle with the capers and sliced chile. Scatter the mozzarella evenly over the pizza. Broil as directed, then cut into 6 slices and serve.

Marinara

PHOTO PAGE 187

¼ cup Pomì strained tomatoes

1 tablespoon extra virgin olive oil

1 garlic clove, thinly sliced

¼ red finger chile or serrano chile, thinly sliced

12 fresh marjoram or oregano leaves

Spread the tomato sauce evenly over the parbaked pizza crust, leaving a ½-inch border. Drizzle the olive oil over the sauce, and scatter the sliced garlic and chile over the pizza. Broil as directed, then sprinkle the herb leaves over the pizza, cut into 6 slices, and serve.

Margherita D.O.P.

PHOTO PAGE 187

¼ cup Pomì strained tomatoes

1 tablespoon extra virgin olive oil

1 small ball (3 ounces) fresh mozzarella, preferably mozzarella di bufala, cut into 6 slices

6 large fresh basil leaves

Spread the tomato sauce evenly over the parbaked pizza crust, leaving a ½-inch border. Drizzle the olive oil over the sauce, and arrange the mozzarella slices on top. Broil as directed, then cut the pizza into 6 slices, put a basil leaf on each slice, and serve.

Napoletana

PHOTO PAGE 188

¼ cup Pomì strained tomatoes

1 tablespoon extra virgin olive oil

2 to 3 anchovy fillets, cut into 3 pieces each

1 tablespoon salt-packed capers, rinsed and soaked overnight in cold water (change the water several times)

7 or 8 Gaeta olives, pitted if desired

Spread the tomato sauce evenly over the parbaked pizza crust, leaving a ½-inch border. Drizzle the olive oil over the sauce, arrange the anchovies on top, and scatter the capers and olives over the pizza. Broil as directed, then cut into 6 slices and serve.

Quattro Formaggi

PHOTO PAGE 189

¼ cup Pomì strained tomatoes

¼ cup shredded fresh mozzarella

2 small thin slices Taleggio

¼ cup shredded cacio di Roma

¼ cup freshly grated Parmigiano-Reggiano

Spread the tomato sauce evenly over the parbaked pizza crust, leaving a ½-inch border. Scatter the mozzarella over one quarter of the pizza. Arrange the Taleggio over another quarter, scatter the cacio di Roma over the third quarter, and sprinkle the Parmigiano over the final quarter. Broil as directed, then cut into 4 slices and serve.

Sausage & Peppers

PHOTO PAGE 190

3 ounces sweet or hot Italian sausage (about ½ large link), casing removed

PEPPERS

1 tablespoon extra virgin olive oil

1 garlic clove, slivered

1 teaspoon salt-packed capers, rinsed and soaked overnight in cold water (change the water often)

1 teaspoon balsamic vinegar

Maldon or other flaky sea salt

Generous pinch of hot red pepper flakes, or to taste

2½ medium piquillo peppers, drained well and quartered lengthwise

¼ cup Pomì strained tomatoes

¼ cup shredded fresh mozzarella

¼ cup shredded cacio di Roma

Crumble the sausage into a small sauté pan and cook over medium heat, stirring occasionally and breaking up any lumps, until golden brown, about 8 minutes. Using a slotted spoon, transfer to a plate.

Meanwhile, prepare the peppers: Combine the oil and garlic in a small sauté pan and cook over medium-low heat just until the garlic is barely golden, 2 to 3 minutes.

Combine the capers and balsamic vinegar in a small bowl and whisk in the garlic and oil. Season with salt to taste and the red pepper flakes. Add the peppers, stirring gently to coat.

Spread the tomato sauce evenly over the parbaked pizza crust, leaving a ½-inch border. Scatter the sausage over the sauce and arrange the peppers on top. Scatter the cheeses evenly over the pizza. Broil as directed, then cut into 6 slices and serve.

Pepperoni

PHOTO PAGE 191

¼ cup Pomì strained tomatoes

18 thin slices spicy salami, preferably from Salumi Artisan Cured Meats (see Sources, page 266)

¼ cup shredded fresh mozzarella

¼ cup shredded cacio di Roma

Spread the tomato sauce evenly over the parbaked pizza crust, leaving a ½-inch border. Arrange the salami over the sauce and scatter the cheeses evenly over the top. Broil as directed, then cut into 6 slices and serve.

Quattro Stagioni

PHOTO PAGE 192

2 asparagus stalks, thinly sliced on the bias

1½ tablespoons extra virgin olive oil

Maldon salt or other flaky sea salt and
    coarsely ground black pepper

¼ cup Pomì strained tomatoes

½ recipe Mushrooms from Funghi &
    Taleggio Pizza (page 206)

½ recipe Peppers from Sausage & Peppers
    Pizza (page 196)

1 ounce prosciutto cotto or other cooked
    ham, cut into julienne strips

3 ounces fresh mozzarella, cut into 6 slices

Toss the asparagus with 1½ teaspoons of
the olive oil and salt and pepper to taste.

Spread the tomato sauce evenly over the
parbaked pizza crust, leaving a ¼-inch border. Arrange the asparagus on one quarter
of the pizza. Arrange the shiitake mushrooms on another quarter, scatter the cremini mushrooms over them, and drizzle with
the truffle vinaigrette. Arrange the peppers
on the third quarter, and scatter the ham
over on the final quarter. Arrange the mozzarella on top, and broil as directed. Drizzle
with the oil, cut into 4 slices, and serve.

Prosciutto & Arugula

PHOTO PAGE 193

¼ cup Pomì strained tomatoes

¼ cup shredded fresh mozzarella

¼ cup shredded cacio di Roma

1 tablespoon extra virgin olive oil

4 thin slices prosciutto

12 small arugula leaves, left whole, or 4 to 6
    larger leaves, coarsely chopped

Spread the tomato sauce evenly over the
parbaked pizza crust, leaving a ½-inch
border. Scatter the cheeses evenly over the
sauce. Broil as directed, then drizzle the
olive oil over the pizza. Drape the slices of
prosciutto over the warm pizza and scatter
the arugula over the prosciutto. Cut into
6 slices and serve.

198

Funghi & Taleggio

RECIPE PAGE 206

199

Bianca & Lardo

RECIPES PAGE 207

200

Fennel & Bottarga

RECIPE PAGE 207

201

Aglio, Olio &
Peperoncino

RECIPE PAGE 208

202
Potato, Anchovy & Ricotta

RECIPE PAGE 208

203

Vongole

RECIPE PAGE 208

204

Pane Frattau

RECIPE PAGE 209

205

Balsamic, Onion
& Goat Cheese

RECIPE PAGE 209

Otto

Funghi & Taleggio

PHOTO PAGE 198

MUSHROOMS

2 ounces shiitake mushroom caps, sliced
¼ inch thick (about 2 cups)

1 small shallot, sliced ⅛ inch thick

1 tablespoon extra virgin olive oil

Maldon or other flaky sea salt and coarsely
ground black pepper

1 tablespoon balsamic vinegar

Scant 1 tablespoon fresh lemon juice

¼ teaspoon finely chopped fresh rosemary

1 ounce sliced canned truffles in oil or
1½ teaspoons extra virgin olive oil

2 ounces cremini mushrooms, thinly sliced
(generous ¾ cup)

2 to 3 ounces Taleggio

1 tablespoon extra virgin olive oil

12 fresh Italian parsley leaves

To prepare the mushrooms: Preheat the broiler. Combine the shiitakes and shallot in a small bowl, toss with the oil, and season well with salt and pepper. Spread out on a baking sheet and broil for 8 to 10 minutes, stirring several times, until the mushrooms are tender and slightly charred. Remove from the broiler. (Leave the broiler on.)

Meanwhile, whisk the balsamic vinegar, lemon juice, rosemary, and truffles, with their oil (or the 1½ teaspoons olive oil), together in a small bowl; set aside.

Remove the rind from the Taleggio and cut the cheese into 8 slices.

Spoon the shiitake mushrooms evenly over the parbaked pizza crust, leaving a ½-inch border. Scatter the cremini mushrooms over them and drizzle with the truffle vinaigrette. Broil as directed, then arrange the slices of Taleggio on the pizza and drizzle with the olive oil. Scatter the parsley over the top, cut into 6 slices, and serve.

Bianca

PHOTO PAGE 199

1 tablespoon extra virgin olive oil

1 tablespoon smoked coarse sea salt

Broil the parbaked pizza crust as directed, but for just 1 to 2 minutes, until it is fully set and lightly toasted. Drizzle the oil over the pizza crust and sprinkle with the salt. Cut into 6 slices and serve, on its own or as an accompaniment to salumi and cheeses.

Lardo

PHOTO PAGE 199

1 ounce lardo (cured fatback), preferably from Salumi Artisan Cured Meats (see Sources, page 266), chilled and very thinly sliced

1 teaspoon chopped fresh rosemary

Maldon or other flaky sea salt and coarsely ground black pepper

Arrange the lardo evenly over the parbaked pizza crust, leaving a ½-inch border. Broil as directed, but for just 1 to 2 minutes, until the crust is fully set and lightly toasted. Sprinkle the rosemary and salt and pepper over the pizza, cut into 6 slices, and serve.

Fennel & Bottarga

PHOTO PAGE 200

¼ cup Pomì strained tomatoes

¼ cup shredded fresh mozzarella

¼ cup shredded cacio di Roma

Pinch of fennel seeds

12 paper-thin slices fennel (shaved with a Benriner or other vegetable slicer)

1 ounce bottarga di mugine (see Sources, page 266)

1 tablespoon extra virgin olive oil

Spread the tomato sauce over the parbaked pizza crust, leaving a ½-inch border. Scatter the cheeses evenly over the sauce, and sprinkle with the fennel seeds. Broil as directed, then scatter the slices of fennel over the pizza. Shave or grate the bottarga over the top, and drizzle with the olive oil. Cut into 6 slices and serve.

Aglio, Olio & Peperoncino

PHOTO PAGE 201

1 tablespoon extra virgin olive oil

1 garlic clove, very thinly sliced

1 red finger chile or serrano chile, thinly sliced

12 fresh Italian parsley leaves

Broil the parbaked pizza crust as directed, but for just 1 to 2 minutes, until fully set and lightly toasted. Drizzle the olive oil over the crust, scatter the garlic over it, and sprinkle with the chile and parsley. Cut into 6 slices and serve.

Potato, Anchovy & Ricotta

PHOTO PAGE 202

2 to 3 ounces fresh ricotta

12 paper-thin slices peeled raw Idaho potato

2 marinated white anchovies (boquerones), cut into 3 pieces each

1 tablespoon extra virgin olive oil

Fried sage leaves for garnish (optional)

Spread the ricotta on the parbaked pizza crust, leaving a ½-inch border. Arrange the potatoes and anchovies evenly on top. Drizzle with the olive oil. Broil the pizza as directed, then sprinkle with the sage, if using, cut into 6 slices, and serve.

Vongole

PHOTO PAGE 203

1 tablespoon extra virgin olive oil

1 garlic clove, thinly sliced

¼ cup dry white wine

Pinch of hot red pepper flakes

12 to 18 very small clams, such as Manila, or cockles, scrubbed

¼ cup shredded fresh mozzarella

Fresh Italian parsley leaves for garnish

Combine the oil and garlic in a small pot and cook, stirring, over medium-high heat untl the garlic is softened, about 1 minute. Add the wine, red pepper flakes, and clams, cover, and cook until the clams open, 3 to 5 minutes; transfer the clams to a bowl as they open. Remove the pot from the heat.

Scatter the cheese evenly over the pizza crust, leaving a ½-inch border. Broil as directed, then arrange the clams on top and sprinkle with the parsley. Cut into 6 slices and serve.

Pane Frattau

PHOTO PAGE 204

¼ cup Pomì strained tomatoes

½ cup grated pecorino romano

1 large fried egg (see Note)

1 tablespoon extra virgin olive oil

Spread the tomato sauce evenly over the parbaked pizza crust, leaving a ½-inch border. Sprinkle the pecorino over the sauce. Broil as directed, then cut the pizza into 6 slices and transfer to a plate. Slide the fried egg on top, drizzle with the olive oil, and serve.

Note: Fry the egg sunny-side up, or cooked to your preference, in a little olive oil while the pizza cooks.

Balsamic, Onion & Goat Cheese

PHOTO PAGE 205

2 ounces creamy young goat cheese, such as Coach Farm, at room temperature

8 Balsamic-Glazed Cipolline (recipe follows)

Fresh Italian parsley leaves for garnish

1 tablespoon extra virgin olive oil

Spread the goat cheese evenly on the pizza crust, leaving a ½-inch border. Halve the onions horizontally and arrange on the goat cheese. Broil as directed, then sprinkle the parsley over the pizza and drizzle with the olive oil. Cut into 6 slices and serve.

BALSAMIC-GLAZED CIPOLLINE

MAKES A GENEROUS 1 CUP

1 tablespoon extra virgin olive oil

½ tablespoon unsalted butter

8 ounces small cipollini, peeled

¼ cup balsamic vinegar

¼ cup water

1½ teaspoons sugar

Combine the oil and butter in a large sauté pan and heat over medium-high heat until the foam subsides. Add the onions and cook, turning once or twice, until well browned on both sides, 7 to 9 minutes. Add the vinegar, water, and sugar, stirring to dissolve the sugar, then reduce the heat and boil gently, turning the onions occasionally, until they are tender and the liquid has reduced to a syrupy glaze, about 12 minutes. Remove from the heat and let cool. *(The onions can be refrigerated for up to 3 days; bring to room temperature before using.)*

BENNO
RECIPE PAGE 213

ETHAN
RECIPE OPPOSITE

JASPER
RECIPE PAGE 212

RILEY
RECIPE PAGE 213

MILES
RECIPE PAGE 213

OLIVIA
RECIPE PAGE 212

LEO
RECIPE PAGE 212

Kids' Pizza

Ethan (Meatballs)

8 ounces ground brisket or lean ground beef (75/25)

2 small garlic cloves, finely chopped

1 tablespoon finely chopped fresh Italian parsley

½ teaspoon cayenne

Maldon or other flaky sea salt

2 tablespoons milk

¼ cup fresh bread crumbs

¼ cup extra virgin olive oil

¼ cup Pomì strained tomatoes

½ cup grated fresh mozzarella

To make the meatballs: Combine the beef, garlic, parsley, cayenne, and a generous pinch of salt in a medium bowl, mixing gently with your hands. Add the milk and bread crumbs and mix gently but thoroughly. Shape into ¾-inch meatballs *(you'll have about 25 meatballs; you only need 12 meatballs for 1 pizza, but leftovers are great for an impromptu midnight spaghetti).*

Heat the olive oil in a large sauté pan, preferably nonstick, over medium heat. Add the meatballs and cook, turning occasionally, until browned on all sides and cooked through, about 12 minutes. Transfer to paper towels to drain. *(The meatballs can be kept at room temperature for up to 30 minutes.)*

Cut 12 meatballs in half for each pizza you will be making. Spread the tomato sauce evenly over the parbaked pizza crust, leaving a ½-inch border. Scatter the mozzarella over the sauce, and arrange the meatballs on top. Broil as directed, then cut into 4 slices and serve.

Jasper (Salami)

¼ cup Pomì strained tomatoes

½ cup grated fresh mozzarella

2 ounces salami, preferably Tuscan, cut into matchsticks, thinly sliced, or chopped

Spread the tomato sauce evenly over the parbaked pizza crust, leaving a ½-inch border. Scatter the mozzarella over the sauce, and arrange the salami evenly on the pizza. Broil as directed, then cut into 4 slices and serve.

Olivia (Prosciutto)

¼ cup Pomì strained tomatoes

½ cup freshly grated Parmigiano-Reggiano, plus a few shavings for garnish

1 ounce prosciutto, sliced or chopped

A drizzle of balsamic vinegar

Spread the tomato sauce evenly over the parbaked pizza crust, leaving a ½-inch border. Scatter the grated Parmigiano over the sauce. Broil as directed, then scatter the prosciutto over the pizza, drizzle with balsamic vinegar, and scatter the shaved cheese over the top. Cut into 4 slices and serve.

Leo (Guanciale)

1 ounce guanciale or pancetta (have the meat sliced ¼ inch thick when you buy it), cut into matchsticks, or 1½ slices good American bacon, cut crosswise into ¼-inch-wide strips

Scant ¼ cup rinsed canned chickpeas

¼ cup Pomì strained tomatoes

½ cup grated fresh mozzarella

1 tablespoon coarsely chopped fresh Italian parsley

Cook the guanciale in a small sauté pan over medium heat until it has rendered its fat and is golden brown, 8 to 10 minutes. Using a slotted spoon, transfer to paper towels to drain.

Combine the guanciale and chickpeas in a small bowl, mixing well. Spread the tomato sauce evenly over the parbaked pizza crust, leaving a ½-inch border. Scatter the mozzarella over the sauce, then scatter the chickpeas and guanciale over the top. Broil as directed, then scatter the parsley over the pizza, cut into 4 slices, and serve.

Benno (Pesto)

6 tablespoons Basil Pesto (page 172)

½ cup grated fresh mozzarella

Spread the pesto evenly over the parbaked pizza crust, leaving a ½-inch border. Scatter the mozzarella over the pesto. Broil as directed, then cut into 4 slices and serve.

Riley (Cauliflower)

1 cup small cauliflower florets (about ½ inch across)

1 tablespoon extra virgin olive oil

Maldon or other flaky sea salt and coarsely ground black pepper

¼ cup Pomì strained tomatoes

½ cup grated fresh mozzarella

Preheat the broiler. Toss the cauliflower with the olive oil on a small baking sheet and season generously with salt and pepper. Spread out in a single layer on the baking sheet and broil, stirring occasionally, just until lightly browned in spots, about 5 minutes. Remove from the broiler. (Leave the broiler on.)

Spread the tomato sauce evenly over the parbaked pizza crust, leaving a ½-inch border. Scatter the mozzarella over the sauce, and scatter the cauliflower over the top. Broil as directed, then cut into 4 slices and serve.

Miles (Broccoli)

1 cup small broccoli florets (about ½ inch across)

1 tablespoon olive oil

Maldon or other flaky sea salt and coarsely ground black pepper

¼ cup Pomì strained tomatoes

½ cup grated fresh mozzarella

Preheat the broiler. Toss the broccoli with the olive oil on a small baking sheet and season generously with salt and pepper. Spread out in a single layer on the baking sheet and broil, stirring occasionally, just until lightly browned in spots, about 5 minutes. Remove from the broiler. (Leave the broiler on.)

Spread the tomato sauce evenly over the parbaked pizza crust, leaving a ½-inch border. Scatter the mozzarella over the sauce, and scatter the broccoli over the top. Broil as directed, then cut into 4 slices and serve.

GELATO & SORBETTO

Man or woman cannot

live on antipasti, salads, bruschetta, pasta, and pizza alone . . . you also need gelato! Dessert in Italian culture is as often eaten during the afternoon, or even as a midmorning snack, as it is after a meal. But if there is one single contribution that Italian culture has made to the international world that is really, truly "made in Italy," it is gelato. There are thousands of places across America with excellent shakes and sundaes and soft-serve and the myriad other frozen dairy variations that we categorize under ice cream, and they are justly renowned for their deliciousness, but there is something about the pure extracted flavor and the delightful taffy-like mouthfeel and pull that makes Italian gelato something very special—and that is what we serve at Otto. It is through the genius of our *"gelataia"* Meredith Kurtzman that we offer here recipes she has painstakingly developed and perfected both in simple form as pure flavors and in the more composed desserts called *coppette*.

You do not need to buy an expensive Italian gelato maker for these recipes—you can use an inexpensive cylinder-batch ice cream freezer. You can buy an expensive table-top model if you want, but the machine is not nearly as important as the components of these recipes, the first of which are magnificent raw products and the second of which are the formulas that Meredith agreed to share in the following pages.

It is always best to make gelato the morning of the day you want to serve it and harden it in the coldest part of your freezer, but all of these gelati will stay in excellent condition for at least a week if they are properly stored. We emphasize that you should use local produce at its peak of ripeness, or perhaps even one day over-ripe, to create the intense flavors that are famous in every city in the "boot" as well as in NYC. And invest in some plastic freezer containers with tight-fitting lids to use exclusively for your gelati, as savory flavors will linger in even well-cleaned containers, and the flavors of garlic or last night's take-out Indian will mar your best work while the gelato sets up in your freezer.

The word *gelato* is derived from the verb *gelare*, which means to freeze, and basically, it is Italian ice cream. But gelato is often way lower in fat content than American ice cream, and it is usually served at a warmer temperature, resulting in a softer, more intensely flavorful product.

Styles of gelato vary throughout Italy, and elsewhere. There are industrial products made with water and flavored powders. You will see these piled high in the display case, wildly colored and full of baubles. Then there are the more artisanal styles of gelato, made with whole milk, real ingredients as flavoring, and egg yolks or cornstarch as thickeners.

At Otto, we infuse, or flavor, whole milk with ingredients such as vanilla beans, fresh mint, and high-quality chocolate. For most of our gelati, the milk is then combined with egg yolks, some heavy cream, and flavoring ingredients to make a cooked custard base, and we let the base mature overnight in the refrigerator to develop the flavors. We have a high-speed batch freezer that chills and churns the custard base very quickly. The gelato is extracted into metal containers and chilled for a few more hours in our blast freezer. Then we put the containers into a display case a few hours before service to temper them; the case is kept at 10° to 12°F.

We also serve a variety of bright, flavorful sorbetti. Fruit-based sorbets will be only as good as the fruit you make them with, so choose the most dead-ripe seasonal fruit you can find. If you will be using the fruit with its skin left on or grating the zest of citrus fruits, buy unsprayed organic fruit. Wash all fruit thoroughly. And churn the sorbet base as soon as it is thoroughly chilled, to maintain the fresh fruit flavor.

All fruits contain varying amounts of water and sugar, two of the basic elements of any sorbet. Some sorbets are sweetened with simple syrup and some with sugar, depending on the water content of the fruit. Too much water in a sorbet will yield an icy, weakly flavored product. Too much sugar will make it impossible to freeze the sorbet. Small amounts of lemon juice and salt will brighten and sharpen up the flavors. Alcohol can be added to sorbet as a flavor enhancer, but it also works as an "antifreeze," so must be used with a light hand.

Coppette, essentially Italian sundaes, are the natural extension of pure gelato scoops and cups and a more evolved and thoughtful way of using the delicious building blocks different gelatos are for the pastry chef. In this chapter, we include some of our faves, which are truly Otto originals, all from the fertile, restless, and creative mind of *gelataia* Meredith Kurtzman. They will knock the socks off anyone you feed them to.

GELATO-MAKING TIPS

- It is best to chill a cooked gelato base quickly in an ice bath, and then to refrigerate it for at least 6 hours before churning it. Even better, let it chill and mature overnight.
- The gelato base should be very cold when you pour it into the ice cream maker. If it is warm, not only will it take longer to freeze it, but too much air will be incorporated in the process, resulting in an unpleasantly fluffy product.
- The gelato should be very thick, with an almost matte finish, when you stop churning it. Then let the gelato firm up in the freezer for at least an hour or two before serving.
- Homemade gelato is best served the day it is churned, but it will be good for up to a week if kept properly frozen.

EQUIPMENT

Here is a list of equipment we recommend for any pastry kitchen:

FINE STRAINER, also called a **CHINOIS:** This is essential for straining cooked custard bases, fruit purees, etc. Look for one that will hook over the bowl or other container, which will free up your hands when you strain any mixture.

MICROPLANE: One of the greatest inventions in pastrydom in the past fifteen years, this rasp grater is used to zest citrus, as well as to grate ginger and spices such as nutmeg.

SCALE: An electronic or spring-loaded scale is invaluable in pastry making—it is much more accurate and foolproof than measuring by volume, using measuring cups and spoons.

INSTANT-READ DIGITAL THERMOMETER: Using a thermometer is the most accurate way to monitor the cooking of a custard base.

IMMERSION BLENDER: A small handheld immersion blender is useful for mixing certain gelato bases, pureeing fruit, and other tasks.

ICE CREAM MAKER: There are basically two types of units available for churning ice cream. One version has an insulated bucket/cylinder that you must put in the freezer for at least twenty-four hours before

inserting it in the hand-cranked or motorized chamber. The other type, which is larger and more expensive, is a self-contained motorized freezer unit. You can use either type for these recipes.

FOOD PROCESSOR: Among other tasks, a food processor is useful for grinding nuts and other flavoring ingredients such as coffee beans, whole spices, and more.

A 2-QUART HEAVY-BOTTOMED SAUCEPAN: A heavy pan is essential for cooking custard bases and making caramel.

BOWLS: Metal bowls are best, as they conduct heat/cold well (and will never break), and they can be used over heat or in an ice bath. A bowl that fits snugly over your 2-quart saucepan is invaluable.

HAND TOOLS: These include heatproof spatulas for stirring custards, a medium metal whisk, a small ladle, an offset spatula, and a set of sharp knives.

ICE BATH: It is important to chill cooked custard bases as quickly as possible, for safety reasons, and the most efficient way to do this is with an ice bath. Fill a container slightly larger than the one that you will strain the cooked base into with ice and a little cold water. Stir the base frequently while it is sitting in the bath so it cools quickly, then cover and chill in the refrigerator.

219

Strawberry Gelato

RECIPE PAGE 229

220

Campari Grapefruit Sorbetto

RECIPE PAGE 237

221

Cantaloupe Sorbetto

RECIPE PAGE 238

222

Lemon Sorbetto

RECIPE PAGE 239

223

Sweet
Corn Coppetta

WITH BLACKBERRY SAUCE

RECIPE PAGE 241

224

Caramel Coppetta

RECIPE PAGE 244

225

Ricotta Coppetta

RECIPE PAGE 246

226

Black & White Coppetta

RECIPE PAGE 248

227

Olive Oil Coppetta

RECIPE PAGE 252

Gelato

Crème Fraîche Gelato

MAKES ABOUT 5 CUPS

Crème fraîche is cultured heavy cream. It's available in gourmet shops and many supermarkets, but it's easy to make your own: Combine 4 parts heavy cream with 1 part buttermilk in a covered container and let it stand at cool room temperature (65° to 70°F) for 24 to 36 hours, until it thickens and sours slightly. Stir it well, and refrigerate it until ready to use; it will keep for up to a week. Because crème fraîche contains a lot of fat, this gelato needs no egg yolks or other emulsifiers to give it a luscious mouthfeel.

2 cups milk

½ cup sugar

½ cup corn syrup

1¾ cups (14 ounces) crème fraîche

½ teaspoon salt

Combine the milk, sugar, and corn syrup in a medium saucepan and heat over medium heat, stirring, until the sugar is dissolved and the temperature registers 160°F on an instant-read thermometer. Pour the mixture into a heatproof bowl and chill over an ice bath, stirring occasionally, until cold.

Using an immersion blender or a whisk, mix the crème fraîche and salt into the milk mixture. Strain through a fine-mesh strainer into another bowl or container, cover, and refrigerate for at least 6 hours, or, preferably, overnight.

Whisk the crème fraîche mixture until smooth. Freeze the gelato in an ice cream maker according to the manufacturer's instructions. Pack into a freezer container and freeze for at least 1 hour before serving. *(The gelato is best served the day it is made.)*

Strawberry Gelato

MAKES ABOUT 5 CUPS · PHOTO PAGE 219

Making a well-textured, flavorful gelato with fruit can present a challenge, because the water and sugar content of fruits can vary with the source and the season. Generally we prefer not to cook fruit for gelati; instead, we just chop it and toss it with sugar and a pinch of salt, to extract some of the water from the fruit and intensify the flavor. Too much water produces an icy gelato, but too much fruit will make the texture overly dense, so we add a little nonfat dry milk powder to absorb some of the water.

2 tablespoons nonfat dry milk powder

½ cup sugar

1½ cups milk

½ cup heavy cream

4 large egg yolks

One 14-ounce can sweetened condensed milk

1 pound strawberries, hulled and chopped

¼ teaspoon salt

Whisk the dry milk and 2 tablespoons of the sugar together in a small bowl. Combine the milk and cream in a large heavy-bottomed saucepan and stir in the dry milk mixture. Bring just to a simmer over medium heat, stirring to dissolve the sugar.

Meanwhile, whisk the egg yolks and 2 tablespoons sugar together in a medium heatproof bowl. Gradually whisk in about 1 cup of the hot milk mixture, then return to the saucepan and stir in the condensed milk. Cook over medium heat, stirring constantly with a heatproof spatula or a wooden spoon, until the custard registers 185°F on an instant-read thermometer.

Immediately strain the custard through a fine-mesh strainer into a heatproof bowl and chill over an ice bath, stirring occasionally, until cold. Cover and refrigerate for at least 6 hours, or, preferably, overnight.

Meanwhile, combine the strawberries, the remaining ¼ cup sugar, and the salt in a medium bowl. Cover and refrigerate for 45 minutes.

Drain the strawberries. Add to the chilled custard, mixing with an immersion blender and breaking up the strawberries. Or transfer the strawberries and custard to a regular blender, in batches, and blend well.

Pour the strawberry mixture into an ice cream maker and freeze according to the manufacturer's instructions. Pack the gelato into a freezer container and freeze for at least 3 hours before serving. *(The gelato is best served the day it is made.)*

Caramel Gelato

MAKES ABOUT 5 CUPS

The best caramel gelato has a perfect balance of sweet and bitter, which requires letting the caramelized sugar bubble and even smoke before adding the milk to it. We like this gelato made with a very dark caramel.

½ cup plus 3 tablespoons sugar

2 tablespoons water

½ vanilla bean, split, or ½ teaspoon vanilla extract

2½ cups milk

1 cup heavy cream

9 large egg yolks

½ teaspoon salt

½ cup plus 2 tablespoons sweetened condensed milk

Stir ½ cup of the sugar and the water together in a large heavy-bottomed saucepan. If using a vanilla bean, scrape the seeds from the bean with a paring knife and add the seeds and bean to the pan. Set the pan over medium heat and cook, stirring, until the sugar is dissolved, then cook without stirring, swirling the pan occasionally, until the caramel is a dark, slightly smoky brown (see "Burn, Baby, Burn," page 248, for how we make caramel in our kitchen).

Meanwhile, combine the milk and cream in a large measuring cup.

As soon as the caramel is ready, remove it from the heat and carefully pour in the cream mixture; the mixture will bubble up. Return the pan to low heat and cook, stirring to dissolve all the hardened bits of caramel, until steam starts to rise from the surface.

Meanwhile, whisk the egg yolks, the remaining 3 tablespoons sugar, and the salt together in a medium heatproof bowl. Gradually whisk in about 1 cup of the caramel milk until smooth, then return the mixture to the saucepan and cook over medium heat, stirring constantly with a heatproof spatula or a wooden spoon, until the custard registers 185°F on an instant-read thermometer.

Immediately strain the custard though a fine-mesh strainer into another heatproof bowl and stir in the condensed milk and vanilla extract, if using. Chill over an ice bath, stirring occasionally, until cold. Cover and refrigerate for at least 6 hours, or, preferably, overnight.

Freeze the gelato in an ice cream maker according to the manufacturer's instructions. Pack into a freezer container and freeze for at least 2 hours before serving. *(The gelato is best served the day it is made.)*

Milk Chocolate Chip Gelato

MAKES ABOUT 1½ QUARTS

We make our own chocolate ganache chips for this gelato. Their melt-in-your-mouth texture is superior to that of chopped chocolate, though you can use that option if you so desire.

MAKES ABOUT 1½ QUARTS

8 ounces high-quality milk chocolate, chopped

¾ cup heavy cream

½ cup corn syrup

¾ cup sugar

1 tablespoon unsweetened cocoa powder

3½ cups milk

8 large egg yolks

½ teaspoon salt

Chocolate Ganache Chips (recipe follows) or 10 ounces bittersweet chocolate, chopped into bits

Put the chocolate in a small heatproof bowl. Combine the cream and corn syrup in a small saucepan and bring to a simmer. Pour the cream over the chocolate and stir gently until it is completely melted. Set aside.

Stir ½ cup of the sugar and the cocoa powder together in a small bowl. Pour the milk into a large heavy-bottomed saucepan, add the sugar mixture, and bring just to a simmer over medium heat, stirring to dissolve the sugar and cocoa.

Meanwhile, whisk the egg yolks, the remaining ¼ cup sugar, and the salt together in a medium bowl. Gradually whisk in about 1 cup of the hot milk until smooth, then return the mixture to the saucepan and cook over medium heat, stirring constantly with a heatproof spatula or a wooden spoon, until the custard registers 185°F on an instant-read thermometer.

Immediately remove the custard from the heat and stir in the melted chocolate mixture, making sure the chocolate is completely incorporated. Strain through a fine-mesh strainer into another heatproof bowl and chill over an ice bath, stirring occasionally, until cold. Cover and refrigerate for at least 6 hours, or, preferably, overnight.

Freeze the gelato in an ice cream maker according to the manufacturer's instructions. Transfer to a bowl and freeze for 1 hour.

Stir the chocolate ganache chips (or chopped chocolate) into the ice cream. Pack into a freezer container and freeze for at least 1 hour before serving. *(The gelato is best served the day it is made.)*

CHOCOLATE GANACHE CHIPS

MAKES ABOUT 2½ CUPS

½ cup heavy cream

9 ounces bittersweet chocolate, chopped

Combine the cream and chocolate in a medium heatproof bowl, set it over a saucepan of gently simmering water, and heat, stirring occasionally with a heatproof spatula, until the chocolate is melted and the mixture is smooth. Remove from the heat.

Line a small baking sheet or baking pan with parchment paper. Spread the melted chocolate evenly in a ¼-inch-thick layer on the pan. Freeze for 1 hour, or until hard.

Remove the pan from the freezer and, working quickly, chop the ganache into small irregular pieces about ¼ inch in size. Return the chips, still on the pan, to the freezer and freeze for 30 minutes before using. *(The ganache chips can be refrigerated for up to 3 days.)*

Hazelnut Stracciatella Gelato

MAKES ABOUT 1 QUART

The secret to the deep hazelnut flavor of this gelato is slow-roasting the nuts until they are a dark golden brown and deliciously aromatic.

2 cups (about 9 ounces) unblanched hazelnuts

3 cups milk, plus more as needed

1¼ cups sugar

1 cup heavy cream

10 large egg yolks

1 teaspoon salt

8 ounces bittersweet chocolate, chopped

Preheat the oven to 350°F.

Spread the hazelnuts on a baking sheet and roast for 25 to 30 minutes, until their skins are very dark brown and the nuts are deep golden brown (be brave!—toasting the hazelnuts to a deep brown is what gives this gelato its intense flavor).

Just before the nuts are done, bring the milk just to a simmer in a large heavy-bottomed saucepan. Remove from the heat and set aside.

Remove the nuts from the oven and grind them to a powder in a food processor while they are still hot; be careful not to grind them to a paste. Stir the ground nuts into the hot milk, cover, and set aside to steep for 45 minutes.

Strain the milk through a fine-mesh strainer into a bowl (discard the nuts). Measure the milk and add more if necessary to make 3 cups, then return it to the saucepan. Stir in 1 cup of the sugar, add the cream, and bring just to a simmer over medium heat, stirring to dissolve the sugar.

Meanwhile, whisk the egg yolks, the remaining ¼ cup sugar, and the salt together in a medium heatproof bowl. Gradually whisk in about 1 cup of the hot milk

mixture until smooth, then return the mixture to the saucepan and cook over medium heat, stirring constantly with a heatproof spatula or a wooden spoon, until the custard registers 185°F on an instant-read thermometer.

Immediately strain the custard though a fine-mesh strainer into a heatproof bowl and chill over an ice bath, stirring occasionally, until cold. Cover and refrigerate for at least 6 hours, or, preferably, overnight.

Freeze the gelato in an ice cream maker according to the manufacturer's instructions. Chill a large stainless steel bowl in the freezer.

Just before the gelato is ready, melt the chocolate in a heatproof bowl set over a saucepan of hot water, stirring occasionally until smooth. Remove from the heat and let cool slightly.

Transfer the gelato to the chilled bowl. Working quickly, dip a fork or a small whisk in the melted chocolate and drizzle it over the gelato, stirring it in as you go to make swirls and ribbons; continue until you have used all the chocolate. Pack into a freezer container and freeze for at least 1 hour before serving. *(The gelato is best served the day it is made.)*

Ricotta Gelato

MAKES ABOUT 1 QUART

This style of gelato is more common in southern Italy—it contains no eggs, using cornstarch instead as a thickener. It has a firmer and less unctuous mouthfeel that somehow makes sense in the hotter climate. We use goat's-milk ricotta, but you can substitute any other type of ricotta.

3½ cups milk

¾ cup sugar

¼ cup corn syrup

2 tablespoons honey

Grated zest of ½ lemon

3 tablespoons cornstarch

1 cup goat's-milk ricotta or other ricotta, preferably fresh

Combine 3 cups of the milk, the sugar, corn syrup, honey, and lemon zest in a large heavy-bottomed saucepan and bring just to a simmer over medium heat, stirring to dissolve the sugar.

Meanwhile, whisk the cornstarch and the remaining ½ cup milk together in a medium heatproof bowl until smooth. Gradually whisk in about 1 cup of the hot milk mixture until smooth, then return the mixture to the saucepan and cook, stirring constantly with a heatproof spatula or a wooden spoon, until the mixture begins to bubble around the edges and steam rises from the surface. Strain the mixture through a fine-mesh strainer into a large heatproof bowl and chill over an ice bath, stirring occasionally, until cold.

Using an immersion blender, gradually mix the ricotta into the milk mixture. Or combine the mixture and ricotta in a regular blender, in batches if necessary, and blend well. Strain through a fine-mesh strainer into another bowl and chill in the refrigerator for at least 6 hours or, preferably, overnight.

Freeze the gelato in an ice cream maker according to the manufacturer's instructions. Pack into a freezer container and freeze for at least 1 hour before serving. *(The gelato is best served the day it is made.)*

Olive Oil Gelato

MAKES ABOUT 1½ QUARTS

Choose an olive oil that tastes really good for this gelato. We like to use a peppery oil, which is balanced by the richness of the eggs and cream. This recipe makes a lot of gelato; feel free to halve it.

3½ cups milk

1 cup heavy cream

½ vanilla bean, split, or 1½ teaspoons vanilla extract

1 cup sugar

10 large egg yolks

1 teaspoon salt

¼ cup extra-virgin olive oil, plus extra for drizzling

Maldon or other flaky sea salt

Combine the milk and cream in a large heavy-bottomed saucepan and bring just to a simmer over medium heat. Remove from the heat.

If using a vanilla bean, scrape the seeds from the bean with a paring knife and add the seeds to the hot milk. Cover and let steep for 30 minutes.

Add ¾ cup of the sugar to the milk and bring just to a simmer over medium heat, stirring to dissolve the sugar.

Meanwhile, whisk the egg yolks, the remaining ¼ cup sugar, and the salt together in a medium heatproof bowl. Gradually whisk in about 1 cup of the hot milk mixture, then return the mixture to the saucepan and cook, stirring constantly with a heatproof spatula or a wooden spoon, until the custard registers 185°F on an instant-read thermometer.

Immediately strain the custard through a fine-mesh strainer into a heatproof bowl. Stir in the vanilla extract, if using, and chill over an ice bath, stirring occasionally, until cold. Cover and refrigerate for at least 6 hours, or, preferably, overnight.

Freeze the gelato in an ice cream maker according to the manufacturer's instructions, stopping to add the olive oil about halfway through the freezing process. Pack into a freezer container and freeze for at least 1 hour before serving. *(The gelato is best served the day it is made.)*

Sprinkle a few flakes of Maldon salt and drizzle a stripe or two of olive oil over each serving of gelato.

Sweet Corn Gelato

MAKES ABOUT 5 CUPS

This is a great summer dessert when fresh corn is in season and you can't get enough of it, but it is essential that the corn that you use is sweet and full of flavor. The natural starch in the corn helps give the gelato its creamy texture.

3 ears sweet corn, preferably white, husked

3½ cups milk, plus more if needed

1 cup heavy cream

1½ cups sugar

8 large egg yolks

1 teaspoon salt

Slice the kernels off the corncobs, reserving the cobs. Break each cob into 2 or 3 pieces.

Bring the milk to a simmer in a large saucepan. Add the corn kernels and cobs, remove from the heat, cover, and let steep for 45 minutes.

Remove the corncobs from the milk and discard. Use an immersion blender to buzz the milk and corn to break up the kernels; or transfer the milk and corn to a regular blender, in batches, and blend to break up the kernels. Strain through a coarse strainer into a bowl (discard the remaining corn mush). Measure the milk and add more if necessary to make 3½ cups.

Combine the milk, cream, and 1¼ cups of the sugar in a large heavy-bottomed saucepan and bring just to a simmer over medium heat, stirring to dissolve the sugar.

Meanwhile, whisk the egg yolks, the remaining ¼ cup sugar, and the salt together in a medium heatproof bowl. Gradually whisk in 1 cup of the hot milk mixture, then return the mixture to the saucepan and cook over medium heat, stirring constantly with a heatproof spatula or a wooden spoon, until the custard registers 185°F on an instant-read thermometer.

Immediately strain the custard through a fine-mesh strainer into a heatproof bowl and chill over an ice bath, stirring occasionally, until cold. Cover and refrigerate for at least 6 hours, or, preferably, overnight.

Freeze the gelato in an ice cream maker according to the manufacturer's instructions. Pack into a freezer container and freeze for at least 1 hour before serving. *(The gelato is best served the day it is made.)*

Sorbetto

Campari Grapefruit Sorbetto

MAKES ABOUT 1 PINT · PHOTO PAGE 220

Use Ruby Red grapefruits for the best flavor and color. Since grapefruits do not always have the same natural sugar content, fine-tuning, using the egg test, may be necessary for the best taste and texture. Remember that liquor acts as an antifreeze, so don't be tempted to add more Campari.

2 cups fresh grapefruit juice (from about 4 medium grapefruits), or as necessary

¾ cup plus 2 tablespoons sugar, or as necessary

⅓ cup Campari

Combine the grapefruit juice and sugar in a bowl and whisk together well. Do the egg test (see page 238) and add more juice or water or more sugar if necessary. Cover and refrigerate for about 3 hours, stirring occasionally to dissolve all the sugar, until thoroughly chilled.

Stir the Campari into the grapefruit juice. Freeze the sorbet in an ice cream maker according to the manufacturer's instructions. Pack into a freezer container and freeze for at least 1 hour before serving. *(The sorbet is best served the day it is made.)*

Cantaloupe Sorbetto

MAKES ABOUT 5 CUPS · PHOTO PAGE 221

Make sure to use very ripe melons for this recipe. Cantaloupes vary in their sugar content, so we definitely recommend doing the egg test for this sorbet.

3½ cups strained cantaloupe juice (from 2 large ripe cantaloupes; see Note), or as necessary

1½ cups Simple Syrup (recipe follows), or as necessary

Juice of 1 lemon

½ teaspoon salt

Combine the cantaloupe juice, simple syrup, lemon juice, and salt in a bowl, stirring well. Do the egg test (see below) and add more juice or water or more sugar syrup, a little at a time, if necessary. Cover and refrigerate for about 2 hours, until thoroughly chilled.

Freeze the sorbet in an ice cream machine according to the manufacturer's instructions. Pack into a freezer container and freeze for at least 1 hour before serving. *(The sorbet is best served the day it is made.)*

Note: If you don't have a juicer, peel, seed, and chop the cantaloupes and puree, in batches if necessary, in a food processor. Set a strainer lined with dampened cheesecloth over a bowl and strain the puree into the bowl, pressing on the solids to extract as much juice as possible.

THE EGG TEST

At Otto, we use an instrument called a refractometer to measure the sugar density of our sorbets. The unit of measurement is degrees Brix, and we shoot for 26° to 28°F for the best texture and flavor. But there is a fairly reliable home trick for gauging sugar content: the egg test. Pour the sorbet base into a tall narrow bowl at least 8 inches deep, and gently add a well-washed raw egg in the shell. The egg should float to the top and, ideally, show a circle about the size of a nickel above the surface. Too much egg showing means the sugar content is too high, and you should add a little more fruit juice or water. Too little egg showing means not enough sugar, so you'll need to add more. It is useful to keep some simple syrup on hand so you can quickly adjust the sugar level—just add it in small increments to avoid losing the flavor you are looking for.

SIMPLE SYRUP

MAKES 3¼ CUPS

2 cups water

2 cups sugar

Stir the sugar and water together in a 2-quart saucepan and bring to a boil over medium heat, stirring to dissolve the sugar. Remove from the heat and let cool.

Pour the syrup into a bowl or other container and refrigerate until thoroughly chilled. *(The syrup keeps for up to 1 month in the refrigerator.)*

Lemon Sorbetto

MAKES ABOUT 1 QUART · PHOTO PAGE 222

Lemon zest and its fragrant oils give this sorbet its intense flavor.

10 to 12 lemons, preferably organic

½ cup sugar

2 cups Simple Syrup (opposite), or as necessary

Zest 4 of the lemons, using a Microplane or other rasp grater. Put the sugar in a small bowl and, using the palms of your hands, rub the zest into the sugar.

Juice enough of the lemons to make 2 cups, and transfer to a medium bowl. Add the simple syrup and sugared zest and whisk well to combine. Do the egg test (see page 238) and add more juice or water or more sugar syrup, a little at a time, if necessary. Cover and refrigerate for about 3 hours, or until thoroughly chilled, stirring occasionally to dissolve all of the sugar.

Strain the lemon juice mixture through a fine-mesh strainer into a bowl. Freeze in an ice cream maker according to the manufacturer's instructions. Pack into a freezer container and freeze for at least 1 hour before serving. *(The sorbet is best served the day it is made.)*

Passion Fruit Granita

MAKES ABOUT 1 QUART

A granita is an easy-to-make form of shaved ice, delicious on its own and a nice textural component for a coppetta of gelato and fruit (see the Olive Oil Coppetta, page 252). Don't be tempted to oversweeten the granita base, or it will not freeze properly. The best results come from scraping the ice every half hour or so, rather than scraping away at a frozen block of ice. After trying a number of high-tech methods at the restaurant, we found that a cold metal pan in the freezer and an ordinary kitchen fork yield the best, flakiest results.

1 cup passion fruit puree

1 cup cold water

2 to 3 tablespoons sugar

Combine the passion fruit puree, water, and 2 tablespoons sugar in a bowl, whisking well to combine. Taste and add up to 1 tablespoon more sugar if desired. Refrigerate for about 3 hours, stirring occasionally to dissolve all of the sugar, until thoroughly chilled.

Chill a small baking sheet or a cake pan in the freezer (the thinner the layer of granita base, the faster the ice will form).

Pour the granita mix into the chilled pan and freeze for 30 to 45 minutes, until it is beginning to freeze around the edges. Stir the slushy mixture with a fork and return to the freezer. Continue stirring and scraping the mixture every 30 minutes or so, until you have an evenly granular mixture. Cover and keep in the freezer until ready to serve. *(The granita can be kept frozen for up to 1 week.)*

Coppette

Sweet Corn Coppetta

SERVES 6 · PHOTO PAGE 223

Catching summer corn at its sweet flavorful peak can be a challenge, but it yields delicious results. Blackberries come into season at the same time as corn, and the two are wonderful together. The polenta cake adds textural interest and reinforces the "corniness."

3 cups Sweet Corn Gelato (page 236)

About 1½ cups Polenta Cake cubes (recipe follows)

Blackberry Sauce (recipe follows)

Cold Whipped Zabaglione (recipe follows)

About ½ cup blackberries for garnish

Divide the gelato among six sundae dishes or bowls. Scatter about ¼ cup cake cubes over and around the gelato in each bowl and drizzle with about 2 tablespoons of the blackberry sauce. Top with the zabaglione, and garnish with the blackberries.

BLACKBERRY SAUCE

MAKES A GENEROUS ¾ CUP

2 cups blackberries

¾ cup water

⅓ cup sugar

2 fresh thyme springs

1 tablespoon fresh lemon juice

Combine the blackberries, water, sugar, and thyme in a small saucepan and bring to a simmer over medium heat, stirring to dissolve the sugar. Reduce the heat to medium-low and simmer, stirring occasionally, until the berries have fallen apart, about 20 minutes.

Strain the sauce through a fine-mesh strainer into a bowl, pressing on the solids to extract as much liquid as possible. Stir in the lemon juice. Let cool, then chill in the refrigerator for at least 2 hours; the sauce will thicken as it cools. *(The sauce can be refrigerated for up to 3 days.)*

POLENTA CAKE

MAKES ONE 9-BY-13-INCH CAKE

This delicious, moist cake is made with brown butter, which can be made up to a week ahead of time, stored in the refrigerator, and then remelted for the recipe.

½ pound plus 2 tablespoons (9 ounces) unsalted butter

¾ cup plus 2 tablespoons almond flour or ⅔ cup blanched whole almonds

2⅓ cups confectioners' sugar

½ cup plus 1 teaspoon cake flour

Scant ½ cup coarse cornmeal

7 large egg whites

½ teaspoon salt

Finely chopped zest of 1 lemon

Preheat the oven to 375°F. Butter and flour a 9-by-13-inch baking pan.

Melt the butter in a small heavy saucepan over medium heat and continue to cook until the butter is an amber brown (use a ladle or spoon to check the color of the liquid butter); do not stir—you want the milk solids in the butter to fall to the bottom of the pan and brown, flavoring the butter as it cooks. Strain the butter through a fine-mesh strainer into a bowl; discard the solids. (You will have about ¾ cup plus 2 tablespoons brown butter.) Set aside to cool.

If using whole almonds, combine them with about 1 cup of the confectioners' sugar in a food processor and grind to a powder.

Sift the (remaining) confectioners' sugar, the almond flour (or ground almond mixture), cake flour, and cornmeal together.

Beat the egg whites and salt with an electric mixer in a large bowl until the whites hold stiff peaks. Gradually fold in the dry ingredients, making sure that they are completely incorporated. Fold in the cooled brown butter and the lemon zest.

Scrape the batter into the prepared pan and smooth the top. Bake for 20 to 23 minutes, or until the cake is golden brown and beginning to pull away from the sides of the pan. Cool in the pan on a rack for 10 minutes, then invert the cake onto the rack and cool completely.

For the coppetta, cut enough of the cake into approximate ¾-inch cubes to make about 1½ cups. There will be extra cake—a great bonus! It keeps well, covered tightly, at room temperature.

COLD WHIPPED ZABAGLIONE

MAKES 2 CUPS

It is important to have the right equipment for zabaglione, and you should have everything ready before you start. You'll need a large metal bowl that fits snugly over a medium saucepan and another bowl for an ice bath, as well as a whisk and a small bowl for whipping the cream.

¼ cup heavy cream

3 large egg yolks

3 tablespoons sugar

¼ cup Moscato d'Asti (sweet Italian dessert wine)

2 tablespoons fresh orange juice

Whisk the cream in a small bowl until thickened; the whisk should just leave a trail in the cream. Cover and refrigerate until ready to use.

Bring about 1 inch of water to a boil in a medium saucepan, then reduce the heat so the water is just simmering. Whisk the egg yolks, sugar, Moscato, and orange juice together in a metal bowl that will fit snugly over the saucepan. Set the bowl over the pan (the bottom of the bowl should not touch the water) and whisk until the mixture is thick and creamy and holds a soft shape, 3 to 4 minutes. Remove the bowl from the heat, set over an ice bath, and whisk until the mixture is cool.

Fold in the whipped cream, and serve immediately.

Caramel Coppetta

SERVES 6 · PHOTO PAGE 224

Caramel, chocolate, and bananas are a time-tested combination, and here the addition of rosemary adds an interesting savory counterpoint. It's very subtle, just barely there, but it makes a big impression.

3 cups Caramel Gelato (page 230)

Caramelized Bananas (recipe follows)

Chocolate Rosemary Sauce (page 249)

Mascarpone Crema (recipe follows)

Pine Nut Brittle for garnish (recipe follows)

Divide the gelato among six sundae glasses or bowls. Spoon the bananas over the gelato and drizzle with the chocolate sauce. Top each coppetta with mascarpone crema, and garnish with pine nut brittle.

CARAMELIZED BANANAS

MAKES ABOUT ½ CUP

2 tablespoons water

¼ cup sugar

1 ripe banana, sliced into ¼-inch rounds

Combine the water and sugar in a small sauté pan, stirring to moisten the sugar evenly. Cook over low heat, stirring, until the sugar has dissolved, then cook, without stirring, swirling the pan occasionally, until the caramel is a light golden brown.

Remove the pan from the heat and gently stir in the banana slices, coating them thoroughly. Return the pan to low heat and cook, stirring occasionally, until the bananas have softened and the caramel has darkened slightly. Remove from the heat and let cool slightly before serving. *(The bananas can be made up to 1 day ahead and refrigerated; reheat over low heat before serving.)*

PINE NUT BRITTLE

MAKES ABOUT 1¼ POUNDS

1½ cups (7 ounces) pine nuts

1½ tablespoons fresh rosemary leaves

About 2 tablespoons canola or grapeseed oil or mild olive oil

1⅓ cups sugar

½ cup water

¼ cup corn syrup

3 tablespoons unsalted butter

⅜ teaspoon baking soda

1 teaspoon salt

One 1-inch-thick lemon slice

Preheat the oven to 350°F.

Spread the pine nuts on a baking sheet and toast in the oven for 8 to 10 minutes, until lightly colored. Transfer to a plate and let cool, then toss with the rosemary.

Line a baking sheet with parchment paper and grease the paper generously with the oil. Brush or rub an offset spatula or a wooden spoon with oil. Set aside.

Combine the sugar, water, corn syrup, and butter in a medium heavy-bottomed saucepan and bring to a boil over medium heat, stirring to dissolve the sugar. Cook, without stirring, swirling the pan occasionally, until the caramel is golden brown, 8 to 10 minutes.

Remove the pan from the heat and whisk in the baking soda and salt. Using the offset spatula (or spoon), quickly stir in the nuts and rosemary until the nuts are thoroughly coated. Pour the mixture onto the parchment-lined baking sheet, then use the lemon slice to spread and flatten the brittle. Let cool completely.

Break or cut the brittle into small pieces. *(Extra brittle keeps in an airtight container at room temperature for up to 1 week.)*

MASCARPONE CREMA

MAKES 2 CUPS

8 ounces (1 cup) mascarpone

½ cup heavy cream

¼ cup confectioners' sugar

Combine the mascarpone and 2 tablespoons of the cream in a large bowl and beat with an electric mixer until thickened; take care not to overbeat the mascarpone, or the crema may look curdled.

Combine the remaining 6 tablespoons heavy cream and the confectioners' sugar in a medium bowl and beat until the cream holds stiff peaks. Fold the whipped cream into the mascarpone. Chill until ready to use. *(The crema can be refrigerated for up to 2 days.)*

Ricotta Coppetta

SERVES 6 · PHOTO PAGE 225

Figs, red wine, and toasted walnuts all pair nicely with mild cheeses, so why not pair ricotta gelato with figs roasted in red wine and garnish with toasted walnuts? The lemon curd accentuates the tang of the ricotta. Meyer lemons have a unique perfume and are less acidic than regular lemons, but the recipe works well with ordinary lemons if Meyers are not available.

3 cups Ricotta Gelato (page 234)

2 cups Meyer Lemon Curd (recipe follows)

Roasted Figs (recipe follows)

Toasted walnuts (see page 261) for garnish

Divide the gelato among six sundae dishes or bowls. Spoon the lemon curd over the gelato, and top with the figs. Garnish with toasted walnuts.

MEYER LEMON CURD

MAKES ABOUT 3 CUPS

8 Meyer lemons or 4 to 5 regular lemons

1 cup sugar

6 large eggs

6 large egg yolks

8 tablespoons (1 stick) unsalted butter, cut into ½-inch cubes, at room temperature

Grate the zest from 3 of the lemons, using a Microplane or other rasp grater. Juice enough of the lemons to make 1 cup.

Bring about an inch of water to a boil in a medium saucepan over medium heat. Whisk the lemon zest, juice, sugar, eggs, and egg yolks together in a heatproof bowl that fits snugly over the saucepan. Set the bowl over the boiling water and cook, whisking constantly, until the mixture is thickened and the whisk leaves a track, 7 to 10 minutes.

Strain the mixture through a fine-mesh strainer into a heatproof bowl and stir vigorously to cool it slightly; it should be warm but not hot when you add the butter. Using an immersion blender or a small whisk, gradually add the butter, blending until completely smooth. Let cool, then refrigerate until cold. *(The curd can be refrigerated for up to 1 week.)*

ROASTED FIGS

MAKES ABOUT 1 CUP

1 pint Black Mission figs, halved

¼ cup dry red wine

¼ cup fresh orange juice

¼ cup granulated sugar

1 small cinnamon stick

2 cloves

1½ teaspoons Demerara sugar or Sugar-in-the-Raw

¼ teaspoon Maldon or other flaky sea salt

Preheat the oven to 375°F.

Put the figs cut side up in a small roasting pan or baking dish that holds them snugly in a single layer.

Combine the wine, orange juice, granulated sugar, and spices in a small saucepan and bring to a simmer, stirring to dissolve the sugar.

Pour the wine over the figs and roast for 10 minutes. Sprinkle the Demerara sugar and salt over the figs and roast for 5 more minutes, or until the figs are tender and slightly puffed. Serve warm, at room temperature, or chilled. *(The figs can be refrigerated for up to 2 days.)*

BURN, BABY, BURN: THE ZEN OF CARAMEL

The challenge of getting caramel to just the right point is to stop staring at it as it cooks: leave it alone, and then catch it at just the right moment—it waits for no one! This is our easy, fussproof method.

Mix the sugar in a heavy-bottomed saucepan with just enough water to make an evenly moistened "wet sand." Try not to splash sugar onto the sides of the pan, as it could crystallize during cooking, and add a tablespoon of corn syrup for anti-crystallization insurance if you like. If you are cooking more than a small amount of sugar, set a lid or a metal bowl over the pan: the condensation created by the lid will wash down any sugar on the sides of the pan, preventing it from crystallizing. Keep an eye on the color of the cooking sugar; when it turns light brown, remove the lid or bowl, if using, and gently swirl the pan to keep the caramel cooking evenly. To obtain a very deep, complex caramel flavor, the caramel should be dark brown, with tiny bubbles gradually changing to slow thick ones, and, eventually, smoke rising from the pan. Now it is time to act fast! Remove the pan from the heat and immediately but carefully whisk in the liquid you are using in the recipe to stop the caramel from cooking any further. Be careful, as the mixture will bubble up. Return the pan to gentle heat if necessary to dissolve any hardened caramel, stirring until it melts, then remove from the heat.

Black & White Coppetta

SERVES 6 · PHOTO PAGE 226

This is our variation on the familiar chocolate/vanilla combination, with a tangy crème fraîche and caramel crema and the crunch and appealing bitterness of hazelnut croccante.

3 cups Milk Chocolate Chip Gelato (page 231)

Chocolate Sauce (recipe follows)

2 cups Caramel Crema (page 250)

Hazelnut Croccante for garnish (page 251)

Divide the gelato among six sundae dishes or bowls. Drizzle with the chocolate sauce and top with the caramel crema. Garnish with the croccante.

CHOCOLATE SAUCE

MAKES A GENEROUS 1 CUP

5 ounces extra bittersweet chocolate (75%), finely chopped

¾ cup sugar

¼ cup water

¾ cup heavy cream

Put the chopped chocolate in a medium heatproof bowl.

Combine the sugar and water in a medium heavy-bottomed saucepan, stirring until the sugar is evenly moistened. Cook over medium heat, stirring to dissolve the sugar, then cook, without stirring, swirling the pan occasionaly, until the caramel is a golden amber color.

Remove the pan from the heat and whisk in the cream; the mixture will bubble up. Return the pan to low heat and stir to dissolve any hardened caramel.

Pour the caramel cream over the chocolate and stir to melt the chocolate thoroughly. *(The sauce can be refrigerated for up to 1 week; reheat in a metal bowl set over a saucepan of barely simmering water before serving.)*

VARIATION: CHOCOLATE ROSEMARY SAUCE

When steeping an herb in hot cream, it is important to keep the liquid uncovered; covering the pan would cause the herb to discolor and wilt, which can ruin the flavor.

Bring the cream to a simmer in a small saucepan. Add 1 fresh rosemary sprig, remove from the heat, and allow to steep, uncovered, for 30 minutes. Remove the rosemary, and proceed as directed.

CARAMEL CREMA

MAKES 4 CUPS

⅓ cup plus 2 tablespoons sugar

3 tablespoons water

2 cups heavy cream

5 large egg yolks

Pinch of salt

¼ vanilla bean, split, or 1 teaspoon vanilla
extract

Combine ⅓ cup of the sugar and the water
in a medium heavy-bottomed saucepan,
stirring to moisten the sugar evenly. Cook
over medium heat, stirring, until the sugar
is dissolved, then cook, without stirring,
swirling the pan occasionally, until the
caramel is a dark, slightly smoky brown.

Immediately remove the pan from the heat
and carefully pour in the heavy cream (the
mixture will bubble up). Return the pan to
the heat and stir to dissolve the hardened
caramel. Remove from the heat.

Whisk the egg yolks, the remaining 2 tablespoons sugar, and the salt together in a
medium heatproof bowl. Gradually whisk in
about 1 cup of the hot caramel cream, then
return the mixture to the saucepan, add
the vanilla bean, if using, and cook over

medium heat, stirring constantly with a
heatproof spatula or a wooden spoon, until
the custard registers 185°F on an instant-
read thermometer.

Immediately strain the custard through a
fine-mesh strainer into a heatproof bowl.
Stir in the vanilla extract, if using. Chill
over an ice bath, stirring occasionally, until
cold, then cover and refrigerate until thoroughly chilled.

When ready to serve, transfer half of the
crema to a large bowl and beat with an
electric mixer at high speed just until it
holds stiff peaks. *(This recipe makes more
crema than you will need for 6 coppette, but
the extra crema will keep for up to a week
in the refrigerator; use it to top gelato or ice
cream or even fruit.)*

HAZELNUT CROCCANTE

MAKES ABOUT 4 CUPS

1½ cups (7½ ounces) hazelnuts

About 2 tablespoons canola or grapeseed oil or mild olive oil

1⅓ cups sugar

½ cup water

¼ cup corn syrup

3 tablespoons unsalted butter

Rounded ¼ teaspoon baking soda

1 teaspoon salt

One 1-inch-thick lemon slice

Preheat the oven to 350°F.

Spread the hazelnuts on a baking sheet and roast for about 20 minutes, until deep golden brown. Remove from the oven and let cool.

Line a baking sheet with parchment paper and grease the paper generously with the oil. Brush or rub an offset spatula or a wooden spoon with oil.

Coarsely chop the hazelnuts.

Combine the sugar, water, corn syrup, and butter in a medium heavy-bottomed saucepan and bring to a boil over medium heat, stirring to dissolve the sugar. Cook, without stirring, swirling the pan occasionally, until the caramel is amber brown.

Remove the pan from the heat and whisk in the baking soda and salt. Using the offset spatula (or spoon), quickly stir in the nuts until they are thoroughly coated. Spread the mixture on the parchment-lined baking sheet and use the lemon slice to spread and flatten the brittle. Let cool completely.

Break or cut the croccante into small pieces. *(Extra croccante keeps in an airtight container at room temperature for up to 1 week.)*

Olive Oil Coppetta

SERVES 6 · PHOTO PAGE 227

We serve a different seasonal coppetta featuring our olive oil gelato all year round, using tart, acidic flavors to counterbalance the fat and salt that are prominent features of the gelato. This is our early summer version, which highlights our local Tristar strawberries.

3 cups Olive Oil Gelato (page 235)

About 1½ cups Passion Fruit Granita (page 240)

Basil Syrup for drizzling (recipe follows)

Macerated Strawberries (recipe follows)

Extra virgin olive oil (use the same oil you used for the gelato)

Maldon or other flaky sea salt

Divide the gelato among six sundae dishes or bowls and shave the granita over it. Drizzle the syrup over the coppette, and spoon the strawberries over the top. Finish with a drizzle of olive oil and a few flakes of Maldon salt.

BASIL SYRUP

MAKES ½ CUP

½ cup tightly packed fresh basil leaves

½ cup corn syrup

Bring 4 cups of water to a boil in a small saucepan. Meanwhile, prepare an ice bath. Stir the basil leaves into the boiling water and blanch for 15 seconds. Drain the basil in a strainer, chill in the ice bath, and drain well.

Squeeze the basil between your hands to remove all excess moisture. Transfer to a blender, add the corn syrup, and blend to a smooth green liquid. Let stand for 30 minutes.

Strain the syrup through a fine-mesh strainer into a bowl. *(The syrup can be refrigerated for up to 2 days.)*

MACERATED STRAWBERRIES

MAKES ABOUT 2⅓ CUPS

1 pint strawberries, preferably small berries, washed, hulled, and quartered

2 tablespoons sugar, or to taste

¼ teaspoon salt

Combine the strawberries, sugar, and salt in a bowl and let stand for 30 minutes.

Taste the berries for sweetness, and add more sugar if necessary before serving.

Glossary

AGRODOLCE This is a flavoring agent—the name translates as "sour-sweet"— we use to balance many dishes with a southern Italian or Sicilian background. We make it with equal parts red wine vinegar and sugar, and just a few drops will add a lot of flavor to anything this elixir touches. To make our agrodolce, combine ½ cup red wine vinegar and ½ cup sugar in a small saucepan and bring to a boil, stirring to dissolve the sugar. Remove from the heat and let cool. Store in a tightly sealed jar or other container in the refrigerator, where it will keep almost indefinitely.

ALMONDS In Italy, you will find two varieties of almonds: bitter and sweet. Bitter almonds, which contain a toxic acid when raw, are used to make almond extract and amaretto. Only sweet almonds are available in the United States. They can be found raw or roasted, blanched (skinned) or unblanched, salted or not, and whole, sliced, or slivered. They can also be ground into almond flour or used to make almond paste. Almonds should be purchased in the shell if possible; otherwise, select those packed in tightly sealed jars, cans, or bags.

ANCHOVIES These small flavorful fish from the Mediterranean and the southern Atlantic are eaten both fresh and preserved in salt or oil. In this country, we most often see the latter, flat or rolled fillets in oil, but the best anchovies are packed whole in salt. Salt-packed anchovies must be filleted, rinsed, and soaked in cold water before using. Boquerones are Spanish white anchovies, which have a milder flavor than most. We like the fillets that are marinated in oil and vinegar—look for them at specialty markets.

ARTICHOKES To trim artichokes, remove the tough outer layers of leaves from each artichoke by snapping them off until you reach the pale yellow inner leaves (the larger the artichoke, the more layers you will have to remove). Cut off the top third of the inner leaves with a sharp knife. As you work, rub the cut surfaces of the artichoke with a lemon half to prevent oxidation (browning). Trim off the bottom of the artichoke stem and, using a paring knife, remove the tough outer layer from the stem. Using a grapefruit spoon or small sharp spoon, scrape out the fuzzy choke from the center of the artichoke. Pull out the small purple leaves.

Put the artichokes in a bowl of lemon water until ready to cook.

Or, if you will be serving the artichokes whole, simply cut off the top third of each one and trim off the stems so the artichokes will stand upright. As you work, rub the cut surfaces with a lemon half to prevent oxidation. Pull off the smaller leaves around the bottom of each artichoke. Put the artichokes in a bowl of lemon water until ready to cook.

ARUGULA Also known as rucola, its Italian name, or rocket, arugula has long narrow leaves and a pleasing bite. Its flavor varies with both type and the season, so some bunches will be more pungent than others. There are several types you are likely to see in the market; I like them all. Some varieties have big thick leaves, others have smaller, more delicate leaves. Wild arugula has narrow leaves and a sharper taste. Baby arugula, with a delicate flavor, is becoming increasingly available. Arugula is quite perishable; store it wrapped in a damp paper towel in a plastic bag in the refrigerator for no more than a day or two.

BALSAMIC VINEGAR Real balsamic is a deep, intensely flavorful vinegar made exclusively in Emilia-Romagna from the unfermented juice of white Trebbiano grapes. The freshly pressed juice is cooked slowly overnight in copper cauldrons over open fires right in the vineyard, to form a thick syrup called mosto or saba. The mosto is put into giant wooden barrels and then aged in a series of successively smaller barrels of different

woods over a period of 12 years or more to achieve balsamic vinegar's unique and complex flavor. The finished product must be submitted to a consortium for tasting, and if it is approved, it is poured into bottles whose shapes indicate the place of origin, either Modena or Reggio—the only two areas that can legitimately produce the real thing. True aceto balsamico tradizionale will cost you at least fifty dollars for a four-ounce bottle and should be used to dress salads only if you own the joint. The supermarket stuff sold in tall green bottles for $3.99 contains caramel coloring and is a pale imitation of the true thing. It's fine for a change of pace in the salad dressing department but unacceptable in the realm of anointing perfect meats or a chunk of Parmigiano-Reggiano, where you want the real thing.

BLACK PEPPER Some of the recipes in this book call for a large amount of pepper. Even if you often use a spice (or coffee) grinder for spices like cumin or fennel seeds, you may never have thought of grinding pepper this way. The spice grinder seems to release even more of the fragrant oils, and it's quick and easy when you need a lot of ground pepper. Pepper should always be freshly ground, whether in a pepper mill or a spice grinder, so it's best to grind just amount the recipe calls for (though if you do have a bit left over, you can store it in a tightly sealed jar to use within a day or so).

BOTTARGA Once known as the poor man's caviar, bottarga is the salted, pressed, and dried roe of either gray mullet (mugine) or tuna (tonno). In Sicily and Sardinia, the tradition of preserving seafood is well maintained to this day. There the long, fat roe sacs are salted and massaged by hand over a period of several weeks to preserve them. Then the roe is pressed under wooden planks weighted with stones and sun-dried for one to two months.

Both types are salty, but tuna bottarga has a lively, sharp flavor, stronger than mullet bottarga. Bottarga can be shaved, sliced, chopped, or grated, and just a little can add a lot of flavor to a whole range of dishes. I love a salad of bitter greens dressed with fresh orange juice, extra-virgin olive oil, and shaved bottarga. Keep bottarga tightly wrapped in the freezer.

BREAD CRUMBS We use bread crumbs in various forms in many dishes at our restaurants, both for coating ingredients before sautéing or frying them and in stuffings for vegetables, meat, fish, and poultry. They also make a nice crust when browned atop a dish or toasted, and we often finish a pasta dish with a sprinkling of crumbs toasted in olive oil.

To make fresh bread crumbs, just grind chunks or torn slices of bread to the desired size in a food processor. We use both finer crumbs and "fat boys"—crumbs that are about ¼ inch in size, which we usually toast, sometimes in a little oil.

To toast fresh bread crumbs, spread them on a baking sheet and bake in a 300°F oven for 12 to 15 minutes, stirring frequently, until golden brown.

To toast fresh bread crumbs in olive oil, heat 1 tablespoon olive oil in a large sauté pan over medium heat until hot. Add ½ cup coarse fresh bread crumbs and cook, stirring occasionally, until golden brown. Transfer to a plate and let cool.

To make dried bread crumbs, thoroughly dry chunks or slices of fresh bread (don't use stale bread) in a 250°F oven, then break them up and process to crumbs of the desired size. Ready-made bread crumbs are available in the bakery department of some grocery stores and at specialty markets. The bread crumbs sold in canisters are unacceptable.

CAPERS/CAPER BERRIES Capers are the flower buds of a creeping shrub called Cappari spinosa that resembles something from an exotic nursery. During their very short season, the unopened flower buds are picked daily just before they open. Capers may be preserved in a vinegary brine or in salt. Packed in brine, they will lose much of their subtle flavor, but they will add a lot of magnificent acidity to your dish as a result of the formation of capric acid. I prefer capers packed in salt, which retain a sweet forest-floor flavor as well as the more subtle sea breeze scent that is lost in the pickling process. The best capers come from the island of Pantelleria, off the coast of Sicily.

At the end of the season, the fruit of the caper bush develops into a drupe, or berry, that looks kind of like a small tomatillo. Sold pickled or salted, these make a great flourish for any dish with capers in it—and show off your super-savvy Mediterranean pantry.

CEPHALOPODS Octopus, like squid and cuttlefish, is a cephalopod, a class of mollusks. Octopi can grow to as long as fifty feet, but the ones you will see in the market are from two to three feet long. Smaller octopus is usually the most tender, but even so, it must be tenderized (see below). Baby octopus, no larger than two to three inches, are increasingly available, and they are very tender. An octopus has eight tentacles, and both the tentacles and body are edible. Like squid, octopi have ink sacs, which, in the wild, can be used to create a liquid smoke screen to hide the octopus from its foe. In the kitchen, the ink can be used to color risotto or pasta.

Many fish markets sell octopus already cleaned, or you can ask the fishmonger to do it for you. Frozen octopus is fine—in fact, freezing helps tenderize it.

Many cooks dismiss octopus as rubbery, an unfortunate reputation bolstered by images of rugged fishermen squatting on the rocks by the sea and flailing away at the poor creatures. I've tried beating them with mallets, puncturing them all over with a fork, and marinating them with an acidic ingredient, but what really makes octopus tender is a wine cork. Cooking the octopus at a low boil with a cork in the water results in edible flesh in much less time, with much less of the toughness associated with OPC (other people's cephalopods). I've heard this is the result of an enzymatic reaction between something in the cork and the protein in the flesh, but beyond that I cannot say.

Calamari, or squid, can grow to as long as ninety feet, but the ones in the market are usually about six to eight inches long. They have ten tentacles, and both the bodies and tentacles are eaten. Most fish markets now sell cleaned calamari. You can buy either bodies or tentacles, or a combination, depending on the recipe.

Calamari must be cooked either quickly or for a long time—nothing in between, or it will be disappointingly tough. Cook it for just a few minutes, or braise or stew it for 45 minutes or so. Squid ink can be used to color risotto or pasta.

Cuttlefish is related to squid, but its body is more oval and squat and the tentacles are shorter. From Mediterranean waters, cuttlefish are much more common in Italy than they are here, but you may be able to get them, fresh or frozen, at a good fish market. The ones in the market are about six to ten inches long, and they must be tenderized like octopus (see above). Cuttlefish also have inc sacs, though their ink is brown rather than black (the Italian name for cuttlefish is séppia, the origin of our word sepia); it can be used in cooking the same way as squid ink.

CHICKPEAS Also called ceci beans or garbanzos, these legumes, Cicer arietinum, are usually sold dried or canned. Like most dried beans, they must be soaked before cooking. Chickpea flour, ground from dried beans, is the main ingredient in *panissa,* a flat pancake served as both antipasto and

bread in Liguria, and in the Sicilian *panelle.* Always buy dried beans from a market with a good turnover; the older they are, the harder they are to get just right when cooking. Good-quality canned chickpeas are available in most supermarkets.

CITRUS ZEST Citrus zest refers to just the colored part of the peel of lemons and other citrus fruits, with none of the bitter underlying white pith. The easiest way to grate citrus zest is to use a Microplane rasp grater. A citrus zester is a small kitchen tool that removes the zest in thin strips; you can also remove the zest in strips using a vegetable peeler or sharp paring knife (be sure to remove any of the white pith from the strips), depending on how you will be using it.

FENNEL POLLEN Fennel pollen tastes like fennel seeds, only more so. It's a "secret ingredient" in Tuscan cooking, where it is used in cured meats and to season fish, chicken, and, especially, pork. Fennel pollen is harvested from wild fennel plants just as they begin to bloom, and it will transform almost anything you sprinkle it over. It's available in some specialty markets and can be ordered online (see Sources, page 266).

FREGULA Fregula, also spelled fregola, is a small round Sardinian pasta made from durum semolina. It was traditionally formed into tiny balls by hand, then dried and toasted; today it is commercially produced. Fregula is sometimes referred to as Sardinian couscous, but it's more flavorful and is slightly chewy. Fregula is available at some Italian markets and can be ordered online (see Sources, page 266).

GORGONZOLA This famous Italian blue cheese, named for the small town in Lombardy where it originated, is made from cow's milk that is inoculated with the Penicillium gorgonzola mold to produce the characteristic blue-green striations. Originally the mold was produced naturally by aging the cheese in damp caves where the mold grew, but today the cheese is injected with the mold and then aged for three to six months. Gorgonzola is sometimes referred to as *erborinato,* "herbed" in Lombard dialect, because of its greenish striations. There are two types of Gorgonzola: dolce (meaning "sweet") is creamy and mild; naturale is aged longer, is firmer, and has a more pungent bite.

MICROPLANE GRATER The Microplane is a rasp grater that has made the task of zesting citrus fruit immeasurably less tedious. There are now many different versions of the original Microplane (and other brands as well); the basic cheese grater/zester is versatile enough for most jobs. Less clunky than a box grater and decidedly sexier, the rasp gives you more control in finishing a dish with Parmigiano or another cheese. We often use a Microplane to shave bottarga over a dish.

MOSTARDA Mostarda di Cremona, also called mostarda di frutta, is a condiment made of fruits preserved in a thick sweet syrup that is seasoned aggressively with ground mustard seed and other spices. It is a classic accompaniment to boiled meats in Lombardy and other parts of northern Italy. Mostarda can be found in Italian specialty markets or ordered online (see Sources, page 266)—and see our recipe for apricot mostarda on page 103.

MOZZARELLA Mozzarella is what is known as a pulled-curd cheese, *pasta filata* in Italian, because of the way it is made: big blocks of curd from either buffalo or cow's milk are cut into smaller pieces and soaked in hot water until the curd releases its liquid, the whey. Then the curd is kneaded by hand and stretched until it has reached the proper consistency. At exactly the right moment, the cheesemaker shapes the cheese by ripping off pieces (a technique known as mozzando, from the verb mozzare—thus mozzarella) and forming them into large or small balls. The smaller balls are called bocconcini or, sometimes, ciliegini, meaning "little cherries." Stretching and pulling the curd gives the cheese its characteristic slightly stringy consistency, resulting from the many layers that comprise the final product. Originally produced almost exclusively in Campania and Sicily, mozzarella di bufalo is protected under D.O.P. regulations; today it is also made in Basilicata and Calabria. Buffalo mozzarella has more flavor than mozzarella made with cow's milk; it is sweet with a slight tang and a creamy, milky bite. It is an essential part of the wood-fired pizze of Naples, and it is often served on

its own, accompanied by a slice of grilled bread (bruschetta) and perhaps a simple salad. That said, some artisanal producers today are using cow's milk for their mozzarella, with slightly different but very good results. Fresh mozzarella may be salted or unsalted; it can also be smoked. Look for fresh mozzarella at an Italian or cheese market; avoid at all costs the rubbery slabs of domestic mozzarella in the supermarket.

NUTS To toast nuts, spread them on a baking sheet and toast in a 350°F oven, stirring occasionally, until fragrant and golden brown, 8 to 10 minutes, depending on the type of nut. (Pine nuts can burn easily, so check on them frequently.) Transfer to a plate to cool.

OLIVE OIL The pressed extract of the fruit of the olive tree, olive oil is produced in nearly every province of Italy. Each has its own style and flavor, which in turn defines the style and flavor of the region's cooking. I recommend keeping at least two kinds of oil in the pantry: a boutique Tuscan or Ligurian extra virgin olive oil, for anointing both raw and cooked foods at the moment they are served, and a less expensive extra virgin oil from a larger producer—that is, a less distinctive but still high-quality oil, at a much lower price—for everything else, including frying and sautéing. That said, in my opinion, you simply cannot scrimp when buying extra virgin olive oil. Choose one that you like for general use and stick with it, but from time to time, try other oils from other areas, particularly when cooking dishes from those regions. Among my personal favorites are Tenuta di Cappezana, Castello di Ama, and DaVero, produced by my friends Ridgely Evers and Colleen McGlynn in Calfifornia's Dry Creek Valley from the fruits of trees transported from my grandfather's hometown of Segreminio, near Lucca. It has a rich and peppery intensity. See page 141 for a list of more of our faves.

OLIVES The fruit of the olive tree must be cured—and, in the process, preserved—using salt, water, lye, or oil, or a combination before it is edible. Uncured olives contain a bitter component called glycoside that is leached out during the cure. All olives start green and eventually ripen to purple or black. Every olive-producing area in the world has its own variety of olives and seasoning profile, and I love them all. My favorites include Gaeta, Kalamata, and Alfonso, but I am happy to try any I encounter. I cure my own each year for gifts to fellow olive appassionati and for the restaurants.

PANCETTA Pancetta, Italian bacon, is cured pork belly. In Italy it is available both rolled (rotolata) up into cylinders and unrolled, or flat (stesa). Here you are most likely to find the rolled version, which the butcher will slice for you. If you are unable to find pancetta, artisanal-style American bacon, available in gourmet markets and some better supermarkets, makes an excellent substitute; www.gratefulpalate.com is a great online source for good bacon.

PARMIGIANO-REGGIANO Parmigiano-Reggiano is the undisputed king of cheeses, and its production is strictly regulated under D.O.C. laws. In order to be considered true Parmigiano, the cheese must have been made entirely in a restricted area that includes only the provinces of Parma, Modena, and Reggio-Emilia and parts of Bologna and Mantova. And the cheese is produced only from April to early November. The rind of true Parmigiano is always imprinted all over with the term "Parmigiano-Reggiano," verifying its authenticity. There are just six hundred or so dairies authorized to make it, following the traditional method: Two milkings from the dairy's cows (and/or those from nearby farms) are used for each batch, and it requires about 160 gallons of milk for each huge wheel of cheese; the average weight of a wheel of Parmigiano is 80 pounds. The milk from the evening milking is left to stand overnight before it is turned into curds; the morning milk is allowed to sit only briefly before it is turned into curd, and then the two are combined. The milk used for the cheese is partially skimmed, as much of the cream is removed (and used for butter or another dairy product) before it is heated, fermented with some of the whey saved from the previous batch, and coagulated. The curd is then cut into tiny pieces and heated before it is finally wrapped in cloth and placed in large wooden molds. The cheese is left in the molds for several days, then it is soaked in a salty brine for about three weeks. Finally, it is aged for at least a year, and for up to 3, even 4, years, before it is marketed.

PEPERONCINI Hot peppers are used mostly in southern Italy. The type varies from town to town, but the word *peperoncini* generally refers to the same crushed red chile flakes we find at the pizzeria. Most of us know our own preference for heat levels—I like a lot. I also like to use fresh chile peppers, especially the Mexican varieties like jalapeños, serranos, and sometimes even super-hot habaneros, in many Italian dishes.

PIMENTÓN Pimentón is smoked Spanish paprika, and it's incredibly aromatic. The best comes from La Vera in Extramadura, and pimentón de la Vera is labeled *denominación de origen* (D.O.C.), signaling its unique status. There are three types of pimentón: *picante* (hot), *dulce* (sweet), and *agridulce* (bittersweet). Pimentón is available in many gourmet shops, or order it online (see Sources, page 266); La Chinata is one of the best brands.

PINE NUTS Pine nuts are the seeds from the pinecones of a stone pine, Pinus pinea. The best are the longer oval-shaped ones from the Mediterranean; try to get these rather than the more triangular-shaped variety from Asia. Because of their high oil content, pine nuts can turn rancid quickly. Store them in the freezer, and always taste one before adding the nuts to a dish.

PIQUILLO PEPPERS Piquillos are triangular-shaped small peppers from Spain's Navarra region (although they are now grown in other countries, including Peru). They are roasted over hardwood fires, then jarred or canned in their juices, and the subtle smokiness of the roasted sweet peppers elevates them far above ordinary jarred roasted peppers. You can find them in gourmet markets or order them online; see Sources, page 266.

PORCINI POWDER Porcini powder imparts a deep, earthy fragrance to meats, stews, and other dishes. You can buy porcini powder at some gourmet markets and online, but we make our own at the restaurants by grinding dried porcini mushrooms very fine in a spice or coffee grinder. An ounce of dried porcini will yield about ¼ cup powder. Stored in a tightly sealed jar in a cool, dark place, porcini powder keeps almost indefinitely.

PROSCIUTTO Prosciutto is salt-cured, air-dried aged Italian ham. Until fairly recently, prosciutto di Parma, sometimes called Parma ham, was the only type known here, but now several other excellent types are also imported. Prosciutto di Parma comes from Emilia-Romagna and is succulent and delicious. Prosciutto di San Daniele, from Friuli-Venezia, has a slightly sweeter taste. Prosciutto de Carpegna, from a small mountain town in Le Marche, is especially fragrant and delicate. Domestic prosciutto is an unacceptable substitute, so bite the bullet and splurge.

The most important tip is to buy your prosciutto from a shop that sells a lot of it—the less time that elapses after a ham is first cut into, the less chance it has to oxidize or dry out. The second most important tip is to have it sliced on a good machine and to have the butcher lay it carefully, not overlapping, on wax-coated paper, not parchment. Prosciutto does not hold well once it is sliced, even if done the right way, so buy just enough for a day or two—and return often to the shop, to help the prosciutto itself.

PROVOLONE Provolone, originally from southern Italy, is the Italian cheese with the greatest variety of shapes and weights, reflecting its ancient origins and deep roots. Each community that produces it has its own characteristic shape. The flavor becomes tangier and the texture flakier as the cheese ages. An excellent table cheese, provolone can be found in smoked versions as well. It is also a good cooking cheese because of its ability to stretch, melt, and flirt with other flavors in a dish. Be sure to buy Italian provolone, not the bland domestic version they slice at the deli.

RICOTTA Fresh ricotta is not really a cheese, but a product of the cheese-making process. Its name means "recooked," and it refers to the fact that it is made from whey that is heated twice. The whey left over from the daily cheese making is heated until it forms curds that separate out and rise to the surface of the liquid. The curds are then drained, traditionally in rush baskets, and the result is ricotta. Italian ricotta is usually made from whey from sheep's or water buffalo milk (most American ricotta is made from cow's-milk whey). It has a mild, nutty, sweet flavor and a drier texture than typical American ricotta.

In Italy, fresh ricotta is sold by weight and comes wrapped in wax-coated paper. If possible, ask to taste fresh ricotta before purchasing it to make sure it's fresh. If it feels prickly on your tongue or tastes sharp and/or fruity, it's not.

Ricotta salata, which originally came from Sicily but today is also produced in Sardinia and elsewhere in Italy, is sheep's-milk ricotta that is salted, pressed, and aged for at least 3 months. It has a mild, sweet, slightly nutty flavor. It can be used in salads and pasta dishes or shaved or grated over bruschetta toppings, such as the broccoli rabe on page 91.

ROBIOLA There are two main types of robiola. Robiola di Piemonte is the name given to a category of soft creamy cheeses that may be made with cow's, goat's, or sheep's milk. These are rindless fresh cheeses that are allowed to age for about a week or so. Robiola di Piemonte is usually formed into cubes or disks and packaged in wax-coated paper. Robiola di Lombardia—rarely available here—has a reddish-brown rind and a much stronger flavor. The Piemonte is the type you want for the recipe on page 129; look for it at a specialty market or good cheese shop.

SALT There are now dozens of brands of great salt in the market. At Otto, we use Maldon sea salt in most dishes. Harvested along England's Atlantic coast, Maldon sea salt is a high-quality flaky sea salt with a delicate briny taste. Look for it in gourmet markets and some supermarkets. I also like sea salt from Sicily, both fine and coarse. I use the coarse salt, with its large, chunky grains, for finishing meat and fish, as well as for sprinking on focaccia and other flatbreads.

SEMOLINA Semolina is ground from durum wheat, a hard wheat high in protein. It comes in both coarse and fine grinds; fine semolina is sometimes referred to as semolina flour. Semolina is used to make pasta and a version of gnocchi; it is also sometimes used in tortas or other desserts.

SOFFRITTO Soffritto is the flavoring basis of innumerable Italian sauces and other dishes, and it is found in many Mediterranean and Latin cuisines as well (the Spanish spelling is sofrito). It's typically a mixture of finely chopped onions and garlic, often with celery and/or carrots, and sometimes prosciutto or pancetta, which is sautéed gently in olive oil before the remaining ingredients are added. Soffritto is sometimes referred to as battuto.

SUNCHOKES Also called Jerusalem artichokes, sunchokes are small pale brown tubers with sweet, slightly nutty-tasting flesh. Despite their name, they have nothing to do with globe artichokes or with Jersusalem. In fact, they are related to the sunflower, and it's likely that their name comes from girasole, the Italian word for that flower—despite the fact that they are actually a North American native. Look for sunchokes at farmers' markets and specialty produce markets. Their season runs from fall into spring, although you may find them at other times of the year. Some varieties are very knobby, others are smooth—the smooth ones are easier to clean. They can be eaten raw or cooked, and it is not necessary to peel their thin skins (though you may choose to do so)—just scrub them well.

TOMATOES A perfectly ripe tomato is a beautiful thing. Unfortunately, tomatoes need to ripen slowly under a hot sun and have a short season. So, while a fresh tomato sauce made with ripe tomatoes may be perfect in the summer, it is always better to use high-quality canned or packaged tomatoes during the off-season. I like two types: Pomì, packaged in shelf-stable pint containers, and canned San Marzano tomatoes.

Pomì tomatoes, sold in most grocery stores, are simply delicious. You can buy them either chopped or strained (pureed); I often use the strained tomatoes for topping a pizza when I don't have a homemade sauce on hand, and, in fact, we use these for our Otto pizzas. Pear-shaped San Marzano tomatoes are a type of Roma, or plum, tomato. The real thing is grown only in San Marzano, near Mount Vesuvius, outside of Naples. They are available here in specialty markets and some supermarkets (check the label carefully to make sure they are real San Marzanos from Italy). I recommend buying these canned tomatoes and crushing them by hand for sauces, rather than buying crushed canned tomatoes.

Sources

ARTHUR AVENUE CATERERS
2344 Arthur Avenue, Bronx, NY 10458
866-2-SALAMI (272-5264); 718-295-5033
www.arthuravenue.com
Cured meats, specialty items, and cheeses

BIANCARDI MEATS
2350 Arthur Avenue, Bronx, NY 10458
718-733-4058
Fresh meat, game, and house-cured meats

CITARELLA
2135 Broadway, New York, NY 10023
212-874-0383
www.citarella.com
Fish and shellfish of all types

D'ARTAGNAN
280 Wilson Avenue, Newark, NJ 07105
800-327-8246
www.dartagnan.com
Fresh meat, game, and poultry

DEAN & DELUCA
560 Broadway, New York, NY 10021
800-221-7714; 212-226-6800
www.dean-deluca.com
Cured meats, cheese, olive oil, vinegar, and specialty produce

DIPALO
200 Grand Street, New York, NY 10002
212-226-1033
Italian cheese (including eighty-five types of pecorino), cured meats, olives, olive oil, vinegar, bottled amarena cherries, and pasta

FAICCO'S
260 Bleecker Street, New York, NY 10014
212-243-1974
Cured meats, pasta, oil, and vinegar

FORMAGGIO KITCHEN
244 Huron Avenue, Cambridge, MA 02138
888-212-3224; 617-354-4750
Cheese, olive oil, vinegar, pasta, and other specialty foods

GRATEFUL PALATE
888-472-5283
www.gratefulpalate.com
Olive oil, vinegar, wine, and Bacon-of-the-Month Club

HERITAGE FOODS USA
P.O. Box 827, New York, NY 10150
212-980-6603
www.heritagefoodsusa.com
Heritage turkeys and other meats (Heritage is the sales and marketing arm of Slow Foods USA)

KALUSTYAN'S
123 Lexington Avenue, New York, NY 10016
212-685-3451
www.kalustyans.com
Mediterranean and Middle Eastern ingredients, as well as an amazing range of international foods and products, including mustard oil and black mustard seeds

MANICARETTI
Mail-order available through Market Hall
Foods; see below
www.manicaretti.com
Imports many of the specialty products used in our restaurants, including bottarga, estate-produced olive oils and vinegars, high-quality grains and rices, and superb pasta

MARKET HALL FOODS
5655 College Avenue, Oakland, CA 94618
888-952-4005
www.markethallfoods.com
Olive oil, vinegar, verjuice, bottled amarena cherries, fennel pollen, fregula and other pastas, Castellucio lentils, and other Italian and international foods and products

MURRAY'S CHEESE SHOP
257 Bleecker Street, New York, NY 10014
888-692-4339; 212-243-3289
www.murrayscheese.com
Extensive cheese selection, as well as olive, oil, pasta, vinegar, and other imported specialty items

PENZEYS SPICES
19300 West Janacek Court
P.O. Box 924, Brookfield, WI 53008
www.penzeys.com
High-quality spices of all kinds

RUSS & DAUGHTERS
179 E. Houston Street, New York, NY
800-787-7229; 212-475-4880
www.russanddaughters.com
Smoked fish of all kinds and excellent caviar

SALUMI ARTISAN CURED MEATS
309 Third Avenue South, Seattle, WA 98104
206-621-8772
www.salumnicuredmeats.com
Cured meats made by my family

THE SPANISH TABLE
1426 Western Avenue, Seattle, WA 98101
206-682-2827
www.spanishtable.com
Piqullo peppers and many other Spanish and Mediterranean foods and products

TODARO BROS.
555 Second Avenue, New York, NY 10016
877-472-2767
www.todarobros.com
Wide variety of Italian and other international products

VINO E OLIO
877-846-6365
www.vinoeolio.com
Beans, cheese, coffee, mushrooms, pasta, truffles, oil, vinegar, and other specialty items

ZINGERMAN'S
422 Detroit Street, Ann Arbor, MI 48104
www.zingermans.com
Cheese, olive oil (including lemon agrumato oil), vinegars, produce, and other specialty items

THE ITALIAN KITCHEN
For my absolute favorite stuff, please check out my own personal equipment (including a pizza griddle) and kitchen tool line here:
www.italiankitchen.com

Index

(Page references in *italic* refer to illustrations.)